"More Than Conquerors"

"More Than Conquerors"

By Paul M. Weaver

*Rod and Staff Publishers, Inc.
P.O. Box 3, Hwy. 172
Crockett, Kentucky 41413
Telephone: (606) 522-4348*

Copyright, 2008

Rod and Staff Publishers, Inc.
Crockett, Kentucky 41413

Printed in U.S.A.

ISBN 0-7399-2392-7

Catalog no. 2564

1 2 3 4 5 — 17 16 15 14 13 12 11 10 09 08

Contents

Introduction: Spirit, Soul, Body 11

Part 1: The Spirit of Man 13
   1. Faculties of Man's Spirit 15
      Intuition 15
      Communion 18
      Conscience 21
   2. Functions of Man's Spirit 27
      Worship 27
      Prayer 33
      Assurance 36
   3. Fruit of the Spirit 41
      Love 42
      Joy 45
      Peace 48
      Long-suffering 50
      Gentleness 54
      Goodness 57
      Faith 60
      Meekness 62
      Temperance 65
   4. "Quench Not the Spirit" 71

Part 2: The Soul of Man 75
   5. The Will 77
      Obedience 82
      A Submissive Will 84
      A Passive Will 87

  Inner Conflict and Indecision *90*
  Always Being Right *93*
  Our Native Desire *96*
  Our Affections *98*
  Faith *101*
 6. The Mind 105
  Memory *108*
  Negative or Positive Mind *111*
  Inferiority or Superiority Complex *115*
  Criticism and Critical Attitudes *119*
  Giving and Receiving Counsel *124*
  Silence in Speech *128*
  The Renewing of the Mind *129*
 7. The Emotions 133
  Nature of Emotions *133*
  Guilt *137*
  Fear *140*
  Grief *143*
  Comfort *147*
  Depression *150*
  Discouragement *154*
  Anger *157*
  Resentment *161*
  Bitterness *164*
  Tension *169*

Part 3: The Body of Man **173**
 8. The Physical Body 175
  Man Is Flesh *178*
  The Flesh Crucified *181*
  Temptation *186*
  Feelings of Infirmity *191*

Chastisement *195*
Suffering *198*
Disciplined Life *202*
Growing Old Gracefully *206*
Victory Over Death *210*

Introduction

Spirit, Soul, Body

"And the very God of peace sanctify you wholly; and I pray God your whole spirit and soul and body be preserved blameless unto the coming of our Lord Jesus Christ" (1 Thessalonians 5:23).

God created man with a spirit, soul, and body in a perfect and blameless condition. But Satan tempted Adam and Eve through the body "gates" (the senses); and through their disobedience, mankind came under the power of sin. Then the order was completely reversed so that man was now body, soul, and spirit—that is, he began receiving his primary direction through the body instead of the spirit.

The diagram at the right shows man as God

SPIRIT **Channel to spiritual world** Intuition Communion Conscience
SOUL **Essential person** **("real you")** Will—to decide and choose Mind—to think and reason Emotions—to feel
BODY **Channel to physical world** Flesh Blood Bones

created him and as He desires to restore man through the redemptive work of Christ. Note that the essential personhood of an individual resides in the soul, and that the spirit and the body are his channels of access to the spiritual and the physical worlds.

The spirit is the "God-conscious" part of man. It is through the spirit that God works in the soul (which contains the will) to govern the inclinations of the body. The spirit is wholly sanctified when it is in complete harmony with the Spirit of God.

The soul is the "self-conscious" part of man. It includes the will and therefore has charge of the whole man. It decides whether to heed the influence of the Holy Spirit from the higher level (through the spirit), or the influence of the devil from the lower level (through the body). The soul is wholly sanctified when the will, mind, and emotions are renewed by, and submissive to, the Holy Spirit.

The body is the "world-conscious" part of man. It is the tangible part, which has the five senses: seeing, hearing, touching, tasting, and smelling. The body is wholly sanctified when its members are fully devoted as instruments of righteousness in the service of God.

Recognizing these facts is of great value to the believer. It will help him to understand how the Holy Spirit communicates spiritual truth to his heart so that he can serve God with his whole being. It will also help the believer to see how Satan works through his body (as well as his spirit) to bring temptations to sin. Let us be "not unwise, but understanding what the will of the Lord is" so that we can be "more than conquerors" through Him.

Part 1

The Spirit of Man

Before man fell into sin, his spirit controlled his whole being through the will of his soul. The spirit in turn was controlled by God's Spirit, and thus the whole of man had direct contact and sweet communion with God. The mind (in man's soul) can never fathom the greatest truths of God, for they are known only by the moving of the Holy Spirit upon the spirit of man.

The spirit is the channel through which the Holy Spirit comes to man; He does not normally speak directly to the soul and body. Man's spirit is invisible yet personal and substantial. Its substance is beyond human comprehension, but we can understand the workings of man's spirit.

Chapter 1

Faculties of Man's Spirit

The spirit of man includes three main faculties: intuition, communion, and conscience. We will examine these three in that order.

Intuition

The word *intuition* refers to knowledge of something without the conscious use of reasoning. It is a spiritual sensing apart from human reason or intellect, an understanding that may come from the Spirit of God or some other spirit. Man's intuition gives him a sense of right and wrong even if he does not have the Bible. Through the believer's intuition, God makes His will known by inspirations and revelations from the Holy Spirit.

Through intuition, there comes a small, unuttered, soundless voice that at certain times inspires a man to live a holy life and draw nearer to God. Then at other times, it strongly opposes what the mind and will and emotion have felt and decided. It is a strange sensation, yet it strongly urges a man to do or not do a certain thing. This is altogether different from some idea or notion that comes by way of the mind or emotion. We need to be attuned to this voice so that we will recognize it when it speaks.

How can we hear God's voice through intuition? The psalmist David wrote, "Create in me a clean heart, O God; and renew a right spirit within me. Cast me not away from thy presence; and take not thy holy spirit from me" (Psalm 51:10, 11). This Scripture and others indicate that God's Spirit will speak to our spirits only if we are cleansed from sin. The Holy Spirit will not work in partnership with an unholy spirit.

Man receives revelation from God through the intuition of his spirit. "The spirit of man is the candle of the LORD, searching all the inward parts" (Proverbs 20:27). The term *revelation* speaks of exposing something that was previously unknown. For example, what do we know about God, the creation of the world, and the origin and destiny of man? We know absolutely nothing except by revelation from God, who has told us these things in His Word.

The Bible was given by inspiration of the Holy Spirit, and now that same Spirit reveals God's will to us through our spirits. We must be careful not to confuse this revelation with personal dreams and visions, for most of these are simply the result of one's former thinking and desires. If a dream or vision is not in full agreement with the meaning and tenor of the Scriptures, it is not safe to follow.

Dreams are easier to come by, and they are often more acceptable to a person than an actual revelation of God's will. This is because the first tends to be closer to one's own inclinations, while the second usually involves discipline and self-denial. Be wary of the person who claims to have received some new revelation through a special vision, premonition, or dream. Often this is merely a camouflage for a will unsurrendered to God.

Faculties of Man's Spirit

Many people search for God's will, but they are searching in the wrong place and in the wrong way. One can have a sudden thought or a burning fire in his heart, or even perfect reasoning, and still be only following his own inclination. God will not be known by man's reasoning and rationalization; He will be known only on His own terms. The will of God originates in Himself, not man, and He reveals His will by the Holy Spirit to the spirit of man. But this happens only after man's spirit is quickened with the life of Christ.

Though God speaks to man through his intuition, that is not the only channel He uses. Before man can hear God in his spirit, he must first hear the voice of God through His written Word. Only through the Word of God can man learn about the holiness of God, the sinfulness of man, and God's plan of redemption. It is through faith in God and His Word that our spirits are quickened so that God can communicate with us by intuition.

God first speaks to us intuitively as we hear the Gospel with our natural ears, receive it with our minds, agree to it with our wills, and by faith allow the Holy Spirit to make it effective through our spirits. It must follow this route, or it will be only an assent of the mind. Many people mentally acknowledge the message of Christ and His great gift of salvation, but they continue to live in sin. The Gospel is no benefit to them because it never affects their behavior.

We need such a strong faith and assurance in our spirits that when we face trials and hard decisions, we can say, "I am confident that this is the will of God. I am determined to do what is right regardless of what it costs." This assurance may not be as real to those who are young in faith, but it needs to grow and increase. "For God is my witness, whom I serve with my spirit in the gospel of his Son" (Romans 1:9).

On the other hand, we must be careful lest we confuse this deep assurance with some emotion of the soul. The intuitive hearing of God's voice does bring a feeling of confidence, but true Christian assurance goes much deeper than the emotions. There is a rest in one's spirit, a sense of "no condemnation to them which are in Christ Jesus, who walk not after the flesh, but after the Spirit" (Romans 8:1). By the intuition of our spirits, we can walk in the Spirit as "more than conquerors" through Jesus Christ our Lord.

Communion

We have seen that God speaks to man by His Spirit through the intuition of man's spirit. Now we want to see how man communicates with God. This must also be a function of the spirit; for "God is a Spirit: and they that worship him must worship him in spirit and in truth" (John 4:24). Our communion with God rises above all our thoughts and emotions, and it even transcends the choices of our wills. We cannot worship God merely by fixing our minds on Him, drumming up our emotions, and beating our wills into submission. He will be worshiped only on His own terms, in spirit and in truth.

Have you ever talked with a person whom you knew was much greater than you? You stood in awe and admiration of his virtues and his ability to express himself. In fact, you were content to let him do most of the talking while you simply listened. This ought to be our attitude as we approach God. We should stand in such awe before

FACULTIES OF MAN'S SPIRIT

Almighty God that we are careful what we say lest any rash words come out of our mouth. "For God is in heaven, and thou upon earth: therefore let thy words be few" (Ecclesiastes 5:2).

Who can stand before such a holy God? We deserve only His justice and judgment, but God has graciously provided a Mediator between God and man. Because Jesus is there before God's throne, we need not fear to come into God's holy presence if we have been cleansed by His blood. Rather, we can "draw near with a true heart in full assurance of faith," at any time, at any place, and with any need we may have. What a privilege!

As we seek communion with God, we must come empty of self and our own ideas. Satan wants to make it hard for us to come to God in this way. He wants us to believe that we can talk with God only if we can perceive Him with our minds. But man's highest intellect and reasoning are incompetent to apprehend God. Man may think all day and night and never be able to reach a holy God or receive His inspired message.

As a Spirit, God will communicate only with His own kind, the spirit of man. The mind is part of man's soul, and it cannot communicate directly with God. Neither can God be found by methods such as hypnosis and transcendental meditation. The mind does experience renewing at conversion, but communion with God must always occur in the realm of the spirit.

We need to keep alive our communion with God in order to enjoy uninterrupted fellowship with God and to know the deep truths of God. If a believer becomes careless in this vital communion, he may resort to using his mind to comprehend the things of God. This may come upon him so subtly that he hardly knows when it happens, but gradually he will lose his spirit-to-spirit contact with God. A lack of assurance will follow, yet that will pass if he continues in this course. Such a one may even testify that he is rejoicing in the experience of God's grace and love. Yet all the while he is only drawing near to God with his lips, and his heart is far away.

The understanding of divine truth requires more than human study; it must come through the light of the Holy Spirit. Therefore, a person who receives his learning only through the effort of man has a faith that cannot stand. He may speak about the Scriptures, but it will be like a blind man describing different colors. We might say that he has received only the outer Word, which consists of the Scriptures written on paper. The outer Word is useless until it reaches the innermost part of man's being and changes his life for the better.

The inner Word is the voice of the Spirit, which illuminates the outer Word and makes it alive in our personal experiences. The inner Word is not the voice of any other man. It cannot be written with ink and paper nor on tables of stone, but it is engraved in our hearts through the Spirit by the finger of God. The inner Word is the work of God in the depths of our spirits and souls, and it will always be in full harmony with the outer Word.

Through intuition, God speaks to man's spirit through the Holy Spirit. Through communion, man's spirit responds in worship, praise, adoration, love, and obedience. This two-way communication is vital if we are to be "more than conquerors" through Christ.

Conscience

The conscience is a faculty of the spirit that the world is at a loss to describe. God's law of truth and right is written upon the conscience of man. It is like the ark of the covenant in the innermost part of the tabernacle, which contained the two tables of stone whereon the Law of God was written. The Law was preserved in the ark regardless of the Israelites' obedience or disobedience to it. The Law was fixed and could not be changed or destroyed. It was the express will of God for all ages and all men.

When God created man, He gave him a perfectly pure conscience and wrote His laws indelibly upon it. God wanted Adam and Eve to experience good and to know evil only in theory; but through the Fall they came to know evil by bitter experience. Now their consciences were defiled, and they could not return to the state of pure innocence. But the laws of God were still in their consciences, always ready to condemn them if they did wrong.

As soon as Adam and Eve sinned, their communication with God (intuition and communion) was cut off; but their consciences continued to function. This is still the state of a sinner today. His conscience makes him feel guilty until either he repents, or his conscience becomes so hardened that its voice can hardly be heard.

Of course, the conscience alone is not a safe guide. It is possible for God's law in the conscience to be obscured by false ideas. Paul testified that he had "lived in all good conscience before God until this day" (Acts 23:1)—which means that his conscience had been clear even when he persecuted the church. (He thought he was opposing the enemies of God.) But when Paul met Jesus, he promptly committed himself to the newly revealed truth of the Gospel and continued to maintain a clear conscience.

The Holy Spirit will illuminate a sinner's conscience with the light of God's holy law so as to convict him of sin. The same Holy Spirit will also enlighten a man's conscience with the light of the Gospel of Jesus Christ so as to save him. If a man is convicted of sin through hearing the Gospel, and he receives the grace of God by faith, he will experience marvelous peace as his guilty conscience is cleansed by the blood of Jesus. What grounds are there for further condemnation, since the penalty of sin has been fully paid? His salvation is confirmed by the fact that the precious blood of Jesus has quieted all the accusations of his conscience.

The Christian must be diligent to keep his conscience clear. Paul said, "And herein do I exercise myself, to have always a conscience void of offence toward God, and toward men" (Acts 24:16). When the conscience is not clear, our approach to God becomes forced because we are uncomfortable in His presence. Such fear and doubt undermine the normal function of intuition and mar our free, open fellowship with God.

If our consciences (properly enlightened) judge us to be wrong, we must in fact be wrong. Let us immediately repent when that happens; we cannot afford to cover our sin and live with a guilty conscience. "For if our heart condemn us, God is greater than our heart, and knoweth all things" (1 John 3:20). If our heart condemns us, can we be less condemned by God, who knows all things and is greater than our hearts? Can the holiness of God hold a lower standard than our own conscience?

Too often when the inner voice protests, people immediately lay plans to quench its reproof. One of their methods is to argue with the conscience and to justify their actions by logic. They suppose that anything reasonable must be acceptable to God and should be condoned by their consciences. But the conscience is not persuaded by argument or reasoning. This may satisfy the mind but never the conscience. As long as the offense is not removed, the conscience will not cease condemning.

A second method is to do good works to ease one's conscience. But nothing we do will ever compensate for disobedience to God's revealed will, no matter how laudable or how profitable to the kingdom of God. Even doubling our consecration and time given to His cause will not silence the voice of conscience. If we continually walk in the Spirit, we will humble ourselves and heed the correcting voice of conscience.

In dealing with sin, it is tempting to take the easy approach and make only a vague blanket confession. Such a confession does not let the conscience do its rightful work, neither does it provide a proper clearing of the conscience. We must allow the conscience to point out our wrongs one by one and then confess each individual sin. Are we reluctant to let the Holy Spirit probe our lives through the conscience? If we draw back from this scrutiny, it is evidence that we have not committed every area in full surrender to God.

Our willingness to heed the voice of conscience will show how perfect is our consecration, how truly we hate sin, and how sincerely we want to do God's will. We may express a desire to please God and mind the Spirit, but this test will reveal the sincerity of our desire. The professing Christian who disregards his conscience is disqualified to walk in the Spirit and will soon be led by some other spirit. But the believer who follows the light that God has already given him will receive increasingly more light and will have an ever clearer sense of the Holy Spirit's leading.

"Unto the pure all things are pure: but unto them that are defiled and unbelieving is nothing pure; but even their mind and conscience is defiled. They profess that they know God; but in works they deny him, being abominable, and disobedient, and unto every good work reprobate" (Titus 1:15, 16). If a person continues to go against his conscience, the day will finally come when he can sin with little compunction and with no grief at all. His conscience is then paralyzed and barely sensitive to God's voice. Here we see another test of our standing before God. If we seldom feel any pangs of conscience for anything we do, it is an indication of a low spiritual state; for no Christian can attain such a status that he does not need to confess sin. An extensive knowledge of the Scriptures, an excited emotional feeling, and strong willpower can never substitute for a sensitive conscience.

God holds the key to man's conscience, which is "the candle of the LORD." He will use the smallest flicker of its flame to kindle new life in a man. A person may despise, resist, and ignore his conscience, but its voice is never completely stilled. It may lie dormant, and it can be deceived and defiled. But every man's conscience is capable of being enlightened by God's grace and then cleansed by the blood of Jesus. Such is the amazing love and power of God.

After our consciences are cleansed from sin and guilt, we have a new access to God. The channel is wide open so that we can hear God's voice in intuition and have communion with Him in Spirit and in truth. The enlightened conscience serves as a monitor of our decisions, and we can "draw near with a true heart in full assurance of faith, having our hearts sprinkled from an evil conscience, and our bodies washed with pure water" (Hebrews 10:22). We are "more than conquerors" as we heed the voice of the Spirit through our sanctified consciences.

The conscience makes every man accountable before God, whether or not he has heard the Word of God. All men will be called into judgment for their use of the conscience, though the ones who have received the Holy Scriptures obviously have a greater accountability. For God has given the Scriptures to enlighten the conscience by revealing His will and His mercy. All who have access to these "oracles of God" will be responsible and will have no excuse.

Those without the Word of God are accountable because they have a law of right and wrong written into the very constitution of their being. God made every man with this knowledge; and to prove it, just let one man take advantage of another, and you will soon see an unwritten law arising, which causes the wronged person to protest. The idea of punishment for wrongdoing is written in the constitution of every man. He either feels guilty and tries to evade the penalty, or he is ready to inflict it when his neighbor violates the unwritten moral code.

But who is so perfectly upright and impartial that he is qualified to sit in judgment upon his fellow man? As a matter of fact, man's judgment is unjust more often than just. "Wherein thou judgest another, thou condemnest thyself; for thou that judgest doest the same things" (Romans 2:1). In other words, the one who sets himself up as a judge is often guilty of the same things or similar things that he condemns in others. So let a man judge not his fellow men but himself, lest he incur the righteous judgment of God.

The function of the conscience is not to give us God's law but to pronounce whether we have kept His law. Because of sin, however, the conscience becomes partial and sometimes allows what it would condemn if it were perfectly pure. There are three kinds of sins that often escape the vigilance of a man's conscience: those known to himself but not to his fellow men, those recognized as sins by his fellow men but not by himself, and those not regarded as sin by himself or his fellow men. Regardless of man's recognition, all sins are fully known to God and must be dealt with when man becomes aware of them.

The spirit and conscience of man will carry every sinful deed right into the Judgment Day. Nothing will be omitted, for the memory of every word and deed will flash boldly into the sinner's face at the judgment bar of God. "For the great day of his wrath is come; and who shall be able to stand?" (Revelation 6:17). Nothing, no, nothing will mitigate the sinner's accountability and condemnation at that moment, for even his own conscience will testify against him. How different it will be if we have put our faith in Jesus! Because our consciences have been cleansed by His precious blood, we will be "more than conquerors" even on that day.

CHAPTER 2

Functions of Man's Spirit

Worship

"God is a Spirit: and they that worship him must worship him in spirit and in truth" (John 4:24). Worship is a necessity of the human spirit and soul. Man must have something to worship, even if it be only a good-luck charm or some other fetish. This is because God made man to long for and reach out to someone or something beyond himself. Man was created for the glory of God; and when he worships God, he exercises the highest capacities of the human nature.

Worship must be in spirit, or it is worthless. Outward forms of worship without spirituality can actually be more dangerous than beneficial. True worship includes a desire for God and a longing after Him. "My heart and my flesh crieth out for the living God" (Psalm 84:2). The worshiper cleaves to God, and God cleaves to him in a double embrace.

The body needs the exercise of manual labor, or it will become weak and incapable. The mind must be employed in the search for truth, or its powers will degenerate. And the spirit must be active in worshiping the Divine Being, or its powers will perish. Then the eyes of the soul will become blind, its ears deaf, its aspirations extinct and useless. Through worship, we come to know the nature, attributes, and holiness of God by faith. "But without faith it is impossible to please him: for he that cometh to God must believe that he is, and that he is a rewarder of them that diligently seek him" (Hebrews 11:6).

In worship, the soul seeks God through the spirit in the highest appeal possible for man. Desire from our side is met with satisfaction from God's side. Worship affords a vision of God, which brings peace and joy to the soul. Nothing else can give the same kind of satisfaction.

"O worship the Lord in the beauty of holiness." This directive appears two times in the Psalms. What is involved in such worship? It speaks of the holy garments of the priests, of being clothed with "garments of salvation" that have been washed white in the blood of the Lamb. These are beautiful garments of praise and adoration, of humility and obedience, of a pure desire to give God our very best. They symbolize a full and ongoing consecration to God as His peculiar people.

The beauty of holiness combines inward devotion with outward reverence. God has a right to claim our homage, both because He is holy and because it is entirely reasonable. Worship and holiness are not limited in place or time. Jesus told the woman of Samaria that neither in this mountain nor at Jerusalem are we to worship, but we must worship in spirit and in truth.

Again catch the reverent spirit of the psalmist: "O come, let us worship and bow down: let us kneel before the Lord our maker. For he is our God; and we are the people of his pasture, and the sheep of his hand" (Psalm 95:6, 7). This carries the thought of prostrating our hearts and acknowledging our unworthiness and our dependence upon God. It magnifies God's infinite majesty, glory, and holiness, and our need to adore Him. In turn, it calls forth a sense of gratitude, joy, love, and submission from our inmost being.

God desires our private devotion and adoration, but we must also not forsake "the assembling of ourselves together, as the manner of some is; but exhorting one another: and so much the more, as ye see the day approaching" (Hebrews 10:25). God made us for fellowship with Him as well as with others who love Him. If we refuse or neglect public worship, we are going against our own humanity. We are denying a gracious provision that God has designed for our own good.

In Revelation, we see a multitude of saints around the throne of God, singing and praising Him for their redemption and for His exalted greatness. They "cast their crowns before the throne" of God, who alone is worthy of all honor, glory, and praise. This glorious scene is a glimpse of the grand hope and ultimate triumph of Christ's kingdom over Satan and all his forces. May our worship of the same God inspire us to be "more than conquerors" so that we can take part in God's final victory over evil.

Music is something we do because of what is in our hearts. Joy in the heart needs a means of expression, so we sing. Singing is to glorify God. It is not designed for entertainment but for edification. Our desires, tastes, and expression in music reveal our character. If a man's song is an expression of what is most significant to him, we can learn what is in his heart by listening to his song.

Music is a moral issue. If we are concerned about right and wrong in our words and actions, we must have an equal concern about our music. The only safe guide for making decisions on any moral issue, including music and singing, is to subject the issue to the character of God. It is certain that some music or singing is in conformity with God's holy character, and it is equally certain that some is not. Music that is out of character with God is wrong music, and we must avoid all such, as we avoid other wrong things.

Music carries with it a power. For the believer, it has the power of the Gospel, but for the unregenerate, it has only the power to entertain. It makes people feel good and helps them forget their troubles. There is tremendous peril in the escalating lust for entertainment in our day. Entertainment has grown to such proportions that it has become one of the major threats to Western Christianity. "Men shall be . . . lovers of pleasures more than lovers of God; having a form of godliness, but denying the power thereof" (2 Timothy 3:2, 4, 5).

Some claim that one of the best means of evangelism is to present the Gospel in the form of entertainment. This is certainly an unequal yoke; the two are totally incompatible. When someone uses the Gospel message as entertainment, he always destroys the power of the Gospel, for entertainment clouds serious thinking and leads away from God. If entertainment dulls the mind of man, it is even more deadly to his spirit. "She that liveth in pleasure is dead while she liveth" (1 Timothy 5:6).

FUNCTIONS OF MAN'S SPIRIT

The words (lyrics) of a song appeal to man's spirit. If it is a worthy hymn, the words inspire a believer to worship God and live a life of holiness. This vital and sacred experience is not at all compatible with singing that entertains; rather, the music of entertainment lulls the spirit to sleep by the stimulation of pleasurable feelings. Satan has so twisted people's minds that they equate spiritedness with spirituality and consider everything unspirited as dull and lifeless.

There is a great gulf fixed between worshiping God in song and being entertained by music. Professional "Christian" performers sing songs of praise, devotion, and Christian experience, and even songs of love for Jesus; but their entertaining nature makes the songs cheap and shallow. Even worse are the sensual overtones of some modern Gospel songs. Christ is portrayed with a romantic sentimentalism that reveals a total ignorance of His true character. This is far from the reverent intimacy of the adoring saint and is rather the impudent familiarity of the lustful lover.

Satan can influence a person's emotions, mind, and will by the rhythm and volume of music. If the volume is loud and the rhythm has a heavy, irregular beat, the music gives an unnatural stimulation to the body. Increasing the tempo will increase the speed of the heartbeat and other physical functions. So-called Gospel music that stimulates physical feelings in this way is not worship but soulish gratification.

Far too many people base their decisions about music on how it affects their emotions, not on its merits in moral terms. Much music appeals to the soul rather than the spirit; and when emotion is in control instead of true spiritual discernment, anything can go. Thus the appetites of the body and soul limit the power of the conscience (in man's spirit) to serve as a reliable monitor. Satan uses the appeal of music as an opportunity to mix the sensual with worship, to mix the half-truths of the half-consecrated with the solid doctrines of the Gospel.

The devil wants to have enough error mixed with truth so that both are acceptable to people. Many know that rock music is off-limits; but when enough "Christianity" is mixed in, it can sound good, feel good, and look good. Then even a well-meaning Christian may not be able to make proper distinctions and to choose the right. The music of our day is unparalleled to that of any time in the past for its ability to charm and deceive religious people.

We especially need discernment in the matter of recorded music. Too much listening to music on tapes is detrimental to the inner melody of the heart, even if it is good music. It is easier to listen to someone else's song than to sing ourselves. Further, the singing of hymns must never become mere entertainment or just something to fill empty space. If one has the habit of playing Gospel hymns while going about his work, will it not reduce the sacredness and solemnity of those hymns?

If we are the redeemed saints of God, we will have a song; then let us sing! And let us make no apology for singing a cappella only, for we find no place for musical instruments in the New Testament church. "Let the word of Christ dwell in you richly in all wisdom; teaching and admonishing one another in psalms and hymns and spiritual songs, singing with grace in your hearts to the Lord"

(Colossians 3:16). The Christian's song is the only song on earth that is whole, healthy, and in tune with the Creator.

Let us sing wherever we are—at home, at work, in church, on the road, everywhere. We need more singing fathers, more singing mothers, more singing children. Let us be a singing people, singing the songs of old, songs of praise to God, songs of unwavering faith in God. People of the world want to hear the songs of Zion. Their songs are hollow and vain, and they know it all too well. The singing of those who are "more than conquerors" can bring comfort and healing to the hurting people of the surrounding world.

Prayer

Prayer is the saints' access to the greatest but most unused power in the universe. Nothing lies beyond the reach of prayer, except that which lies outside the will of God. "Prayer is the burden of a sigh, / The falling of a tear, / The upward glancing of the eye, / When none but God is near." True, fervent prayer is the life-giving oxygen of vital Christianity.

When we feel too busy to pray, let us take time to pray. Let prayer be the key of the morning and the bolt of the evening. If our day is hemmed with prayer, it is less likely to unravel. Daily prayers are the best cure for daily cares. God does not always send us what we want, but He promises to supply all our needs.

Prayer is the best communication system ever designed. When President Nixon spoke with the astronauts on the moon, it was the greatest thing man had ever accomplished in the field of communication. But prayer is far greater than all this. Prayer is the creature on earth communicating with the Creator in heaven. Yet prayer never attains its full potential when it can be set in human words. Prayer reaches its greatest intensity when it is no more than a voiceless cry: "Lord, help me."

There is tremendous power in prayer. This does not mean power to wear down God's resistance or to manipulate Him into doing what we want, for the Lord delights in hearing our prayers. "If ye then, being evil, know how to give good gifts unto your children, how much more shall your Father which is in heaven give good things to them that ask him?" (Matthew 7:11). The power of prayer is the mighty power of God released to answer the petitions of His children.

Prayer becomes powerful when we practice it regularly. There is a natural tendency of neglecting to pray. We may say, "Lord, teach us *how* to pray," when we should be saying, "Lord, teach us *to pray*." For no matter how excellent our ability in prayer, it will do little good if we seldom pray.

Prayer becomes powerful when it rises from a humble, helpless heart. As the apostle Paul said, "When I am weak, then am I strong." Too often we are self-sufficient and not even aware of how inadequate we are. But when we sense our utter helplessness, our petition becomes an "effectual fervent prayer," which has great power with God.

Prayer becomes powerful when we pray according to God's will and leave the choice with Him as to how He shall answer. This gives God the freedom to do what He wanted to do all along, but was hindered because we were in the way. God often waits to act until the Christian prays, and then He does things that He would not have done otherwise. How many things in life depend on our prayers in submission to His will!

Prayer becomes powerful when we rise above our own selfishness and seek the welfare of others. Even a very good request may have a selfish motive behind it. We need to stop using prayer as a way to surround ourselves with comfort or to have God run our errands, and start using it to seek blessings for others. If we make ourselves available, God is likely to provide us with the means and the grace to answer our own prayers. Then our prayers will have power indeed.

We must never underestimate the need and the power of intercessory prayer. Let us pray for our families, for our fellow believers, for our ministers, and for our Christian schoolteachers. Let us pray for those who fail to pray for themselves, and bring them and their circumstances under the mighty power of God. In no way can we exert a stronger influence on other people's lives.

May our prayers be mixed with faith. May we turn every care over to God. May we rid ourselves of any inward feelings of resentment, ill will, or revenge that will cancel the power of our prayers. May we individually and collectively bend ourselves before God and claim the promise that He will bend to hear our prayers. God is waiting to show Himself strong when He sees that we are fully devoted to Him.

Jesus was perfect, yet He needed to pray. He prayed that the power of God would come down from heaven and assist Him as He passed through the trials and temptations of His human experience. Others may never know how much we pray, but they will see the power of God that comes into our lives through prayer. They will see the fervency of our obedience to God's Word. They will see the magnitude and intensity of our love for the brethren and for all men.

Prayer is so simple. It is like quietly opening a door and slipping into the presence of God. Prayer releases the energies of God, for it asks God to do what we cannot do ourselves. A life without prayer is like a house without nails: prayer holds our lives together. We will be "more than conquerors" in proportion to our diligence in prayer. Come and let us pray.

Assurance

The quest of all men is to find something or someone in whom they can find rest, confidence, and security. That quest ends only in God, in His eternal promises and provisions of grace. To find God is not a quest of the intellect but of the heart and spirit of man. The conscience is never at rest until it finds peace with God.

The Christian needs a firm persuasion of his own salvation, a certitude with respect to the question of whether he is right with God. The degree of assurance that a person may have is a disputed question. One extreme is to think there can be no assurance until death, and the other extreme is to think there is no possibility of being lost after receiving salvation. Somewhere in between, there must be a settled fact of Christian assurance.

The idea that one can have assurance only after death is not true Christian assurance. Of course, there is always the possibility of falling into sin and voluntarily departing from Christ. But if we cling to God in true faith, we will find His provisions and promises well sufficient to carry us through to the end. The penitent, obedient child of God can claim assurance and have peace in his soul every moment of his life even until death. Assurance should be the common privilege of all true believers.

The idea that one can have assurance while living in sin is also not true Christian assurance. It is an illusion in fact as well as experience, for how can one have real peace with God while doing what he knows God hates? This fallacy is directly related to the Calvinist doctrine of unconditional eternal security. But even that security is not as solid as it is often portrayed. According to eternal-security people, if a man becomes a Christian and later returns to a life of sin, it shows that he was never saved to start with. That kind of assurance is no better than believing that one can lose his salvation.

Assurance of salvation begins as we simply believe the promises of God. It is confirmed by the Holy Spirit Himself, who "beareth witness with our spirit, that we are the children of God" (Romans 8:16). The witness of the Spirit brings faith to its full development and issues into a joyous experience of new life in Christ. It leads to a full assurance of faith and provides a solid hope, "which hope we have as an anchor of the soul, both sure and stedfast" (Hebrews 6:19). This is true Christian assurance.

Faith and hope are closely related. Faith is our confidence in Christ for salvation as it relates to the past and present, and hope is our confidence in Him as it relates to the future. Hope is much more than wishful thinking. It is an active principle of life, which is grounded in the character and Word of God. Christian hope is such that we can have confidence even when all natural conditions are to the contrary. It is like the experience of Abraham, "who against hope believed in hope" that God would give him a son, even though he and Sarah were old. The Christian also rests his hope on the unfailing promises of God.

Our assurance is strengthened by the tests and trials of life. These experiences are of such a nature that they prove the vanity and emptiness of worldly things, and they drive us to the hope of a higher and better life. As we win victories over our own self-will and sinful desires, we receive the joy and rest of Christian assurance. One victory gives hope of more to follow, and thus our present assurance builds upon past assurances.

Hope and assurance purify the heart. They inspire a willingness to bear the chastening of the Lord, which afterward yields "the peaceable fruit of righteousness" (Hebrews 12:11). Our hope of heaven leads to personal purity (the putting away of sin and fleshly lusts) in anticipation of meeting the Lord. The prospect of being like Jesus someday in glory gives us a desire to have a character like His, here and now.

Three F's have vital importance in the Christian experience. They are the *facts* about Jesus Christ and His redemptive work, the *faith* we must exercise to receive salvation and enabling grace, and the *feelings* we experience as we go through life. Each of these must be in its proper place if we are to have Christian assurance.

The *facts* are clear and simple. God is holy, man is sinful, and Jesus is the only Mediator between God and man. We must repent and believe in Jesus to be reconciled to God. These and related facts form a solid base for our salvation, which will always remain even if our faith becomes weak or our feelings go awry.

We need *faith* before these facts will do us any good. When we receive Jesus, we must actually believe that we now have salvation—believe it as fully as if we had a certificate signed by God Himself. When we are justified by faith, we must believe that God has declared us righteous—be as convinced as if we had heard His voice speaking audibly. This kind of conviction needs to characterize our whole outlook on God and His Word. Anything less is not true faith and will not bring real assurance of salvation.

Genuine faith based on Bible facts often brings *feelings* of great joy, especially at first. But feelings must never be the source of our assurance. Feelings depend on circumstances and are therefore a source of insecurity rather than assurance. For example, if we have a high fever, we will feel miserable regardless of our spiritual condition. God has given us the witness of His Spirit so that we can have assurance of salvation in any circumstances. Faith must always take precedence over feelings.

It is possible for a true believer to be unaware or forgetful of his spiritual wealth. He may have eternal life and not feel sure of it. Have we not known a devout believer who lived in uncertainty through wondering whether God really accepted him? And even if we usually live in the sunshine of God's love, there are times when our joys seem clouded over. At such times we need to remind ourselves of the facts and rest our faith on them instead of our feelings.

It is also possible to be deceived by good feelings. Some people talk much about their close relationship with God, their peace and joy, and even about the Spirit's special revelations to them. Their feeling of assurance may be ever so real; but they do not have victory over sin, nor do they forsake worldly pleasures and follow Christ wholeheartedly. This is a false assurance based on feelings, which are a foundation of straw.

Our spiritual lives have not blossomed into their full beauty until we are perfectly at home in the love of God in Christ, and we step as confidently there as children do in their parents' home. The question of whether we are truly God's children should never come up, as long as we meet the conditions. "And he that keepeth his commandments dwelleth in him, and he in him. And hereby we know that he abideth in us, by the Spirit which he hath given us" (1 John 3:24). The full assurance of God's favor and blessing will enable us to go forth as "more than conquerors" for Him.

CHAPTER 3

Fruit of the Spirit

"But the fruit of the Spirit is love, joy, peace, long-suffering, gentleness, goodness, faith, meekness, temperance: against such there is no law" (Galatians 5:22, 23). Here we have a picture of a lovely garden with all the choicest produce of the Spirit. The graces named are in direct contrast to the works of the flesh, which are confused and conflicting. One lust contends with another for the mastery. But the fruit of the Spirit is like well-formed fruit, with no part competing against another in its growing. Each grace contributes to the richness and beauty of the whole. All are consistent.

The apostle wrote of the nine as together constituting the fruit of the Spirit, implying that all nine graces are needed to make the fruit complete. Christian character must be fully and harmoniously developed. The absence of any part mars the perfection of the whole. Although the graces of the Christian life grow out of the indwelling of the Spirit of God, they also need to be directly and individually cultivated to bring about the desired consistency.

There is a law against the seventeen works of the flesh, to condemn them; but there is no law to restrain the nine graces of the Spirit. We have unlimited freedom to be "fruitful in every good work, and increasing in the knowledge of God" (Colossians 1:10).

Love

The first three graces are love, joy, and peace. These all spring out of the believer's relationship with Christ. Self-sacrificing love issues into joy, and peace is the result of both love and joy. Love is the tie that binds our hearts to God; joy is the glad emotion that springs up after we are reconciled; peace is the summer calm of the soul that has entered into its rest. Love is the foundation, joy is the superstructure, and peace is the crowning pinnacle of the whole.

The fact that love comes first matches Paul's emphasis in 1 Corinthians 13 and his statement in Romans 13:10: "Love worketh no ill to his neighbour: therefore love is the fulfilling of the law." The principle of love is not an arbitrary condition imposed on believers; it is an integral part of Christianity. Neither is it an occasional attitude manifested toward those who love us, but a characteristic attitude of life. If love is lacking; everything is lacking. If we are immature in love, we are immature as Christians.

Knowledge may make a man look big, but only love can make him grow to his full stature in Christ. Men may know everything about life except how to live it. They can pick life to pieces but do not know how to put it back together. People have been probing themselves for many years, trying to analyze their problems and find solutions. Their problems could be solved and dissolved if only they could find the depths of love in God and their fellow men.

There are two ways to get rid of a block of ice. One is to smash it with a hammer, in which case you succeed only in scattering it, not in destroying it. The other way is to melt it, in which case you really do get rid of it. Jesus on the cross was God, not smashing His enemies, but seeking to melt them. The only good way to get rid of our enemies is to turn them into friends. The only possible way to do this is by loving them.

We need to make love our aim, our life purpose. This will take the exercise of love out of the occasional and spasmodic, and will make it the central controlling power in our lives. "Charity never faileth" because it always seeks ways to express itself; and when it does so, it will always succeed. For in expressing love, you will become more loving even if the other person refuses the love expressed. You will be fulfilling your purpose in life because you have become a more loving person.

There is room for competition in showing love one to another. This is suggested in 1 Thessalonians 3:12, which tells us to "increase and abound [excel] in love one toward another." Seeking to excel in love is not only constructive to others but also rewarding to us. It will strengthen, establish, and prove us "unblameable in holiness before God, . . . at the coming of our Lord Jesus Christ" (1 Thessalonians 3:13).

The pattern for our loving is God. He loves us not merely for what we are but for what He sees we can be. And we should have the same kind of love for others. God, by His love, tends to mold us into the persons He wants us to be; and through His love, we in turn can love our fellow men into being what they should be. True Christian love does not depend on a return; therefore, it can be invulnerable to the lack of appreciation. We need not strain to love, but simply let the love of God flow through us to others (1 John 4:11). As God's love dwells in us, He perfects our love and perfects us in the process.

Broadcasting love in general is a good attitude, but it can become a cheap substitute for extending love in particular. It costs only sentiment to love in general, but it can cost dearly to love in particular. Find some particular person with a particular need, shed your beams of love upon him, and you will be blessed for so doing. You may be afraid of certain people; however, "there is no fear in love; but perfect love casteth out fear" (1 John 4:18). So do not fight your fears; go out and love, and you will soon find that love has dissolved your fears.

Love can take place only where there is self-surrender. If we hold on to self, love cannot have its perfect liberty. This applies to our love for God as well as our fellow men. We cannot truly love God or others unless we surrender our own selfish desires. Love is an emancipating passion, for it breaks the tyranny of self-preoccupation and frees our powers to operate outside ourselves. The result is deep satisfaction because we are fulfilling the purpose for which God made us.

Since true love is expressed in sacrifice, it is not an easy way of life. But love can take on impossible tasks and lighten loads that one could never carry otherwise. Nothing is hard if done for love's sake. The yoke of love is easy; the yoke of duty is hard. There is a world of difference between acting from love and acting from duty. The task may be the same; but love makes everything light, while duty makes everything drudgery. Loveless living is a hard way indeed.

May the grace of love grow in us abundantly until our Lord's return, and then we will know love in its perfection.

Joy

Everybody wants to be happy, but many people are intensely unhappy. For one thing, they seek happiness in external pursuits. True joy comes from inner relationships, not from happenings. Why do so many people ruin their lives in pursuing sinful pleasures? It is because they want to forget the emptiness of their lives, or forget their guilt, or escape their inner and outer conflicts.

The Christian does not want to forget his emptiness; he rejoices in his fullness of life. He does not want to forget his former guilt; he remembers with joy his divine forgiveness. He does not try to escape his conflicts; he has learned to let the Lord deal with them. The believer has the joy of knowing that God approves of him and that God will sustain him no matter what happens.

Joy is one of the central characteristics of the Christian. Yet far too many professing Christians know too little of real joy; they find themselves under the lash of duty rather than unabashed delight. Some do not even expect joy, for they have lived in their gloom so long that they feel it is the assigned lot of the Christian. They almost creak in soul and body on their supposed way to glory. Joy seems like a luxury to them rather than a normal experience.

But the Scriptures say, "Rejoice evermore" (1 Thessalonians 5:16). Our heavenly Father is one "who giveth us richly all things to enjoy" (1 Timothy 6:17). We can grow in character and in joy even under the lash. If there is no other reason for joy, we can at least rejoice in our own growth. Let us enjoy the peace we have with God (Romans 5:1). Let us enjoy our redemption. Let us enjoy our "access by one Spirit unto the Father" (Ephesians 2:18). We can thank God for everything if we see God in everything.

"Your life is hid with Christ in God" (Colossians 3:3). The Christian's spring of joy is hidden within, out of sight from the world. It never runs dry, for it is deep in God. The Christian rejoices not in what he possesses, nor in what he does, nor in what others do for him. His joy abides in his living relationship with God, apart from the flux of possession and nonpossession, of success and failure, of good treatment and ill treatment. The Christian can do without anything on earth—even life on earth—because he has eternal life now, which is rooted in eternity and the eternal God.

There are two ways to be rich: one is in the abundance of your possessions, and the other is in the fewness of your wants. Jesus said, "Foxes have holes, and birds of the air have nests; but the Son of man hath not where to lay his head" (Luke 9:58). His joy was not in His circumstances but in His relationship with the Father. The Christian's joy results from a sense of well-being, acceptance, and harmony with Jesus Christ. He alone can give us an ultimate, unshakable, immeasurable, eternal joy that continues after all earthly joys are silent and gone.

If we are gloomy, something is wrong—our joy is blocked. Of course, feelings of despondency may come because of adverse circumstances. But aside from that, do not look around for the cause; look within. If our joy is centered in this thing, that thing, or some other thing, we are doomed to disappointment. Jesus Christ is the only one we can depend on for joy; anything else is a staff that, if one leans too hard, will break and pierce the hand and heart.

If Christ is going to make the total you joyful, He must have you totally. Surrender yourself and all your sorrows and gloom to God. Make sure you hold no areas in reserve; more failures come at this point than at any other. Compromise causes many people's joy to flounder. We tend to give some and to withhold some; but the things withheld disturb our rest, and our joy dies.

Many think they will have life at its best if they can have everything their hearts desire. Judas got what he wanted; then after he got it, he despised it and threw it down. We too will despise anything we take in the place of Christ: we will inwardly or outwardly throw it down. There are two tragedies in life: one is not to obtain the heart's desire, and the other is to obtain it. Getting our own way instead of God's will is indeed a great tragedy for us. Anything we pursue against His desire is a delusion that will turn to gravel in the mouth.

There are many who build their lives on the flesh instead of the spirit; but then the years come and go, and the flesh is unable to sustain the pleasure any longer. Finally it fades completely, and all that remains is the memory of sensual living with its echo of emptiness and disappointment. A sad case indeed is a person who has gained wealth, fame, or some other desire of his heart but has not found fulfillment—only leanness of soul. In contrast, our joy in Christ can grow richer in content, purer in intent, and broader in extent.

Joy is God's gift to us, and having received it, we must freely give. When we share joy with others, it multiplies in our hands like the loaves and fish in the hands of Jesus. We give five loaves and two fish, and we gather up twelve baskets of joy. The happiest people are those who deliberately take on themselves sorrow, pain, and even hardship in the behalf of others. Then in the midst of their labor, they catch a strange, deep joy that words are not able to express. Too many people feel they have a right to be happy and the world owes it to them. This kind of individual is always unhappy.

By the grace of God, let us allow Christ to fill our inner springs with living water. Let us replace our long faces with a cheerful countenance, and our gloomy words with songs of joy. "Therefore with joy shall ye draw water out of the wells of salvation" (Isaiah 12:3). The cup that is filled with sweet joy will never spill out bitterness, no matter how hard it is knocked.

Peace

It is not without purpose in the inspired order that love is pre-eminent, followed by the delight of joy and then the quietness of peace. Peace is joy with its arms folded in serene assurance. The peace of the Spirit is much more than what is commonly called peace of mind. You cannot have true peace of mind if you have conflict in your spirit. But as peace with God rules in the depths of your spirit, peace of mind will surely follow.

To tinker with the mind and leave the depths untouched

is a serious deception that may rob us of the very ability to obtain true peace. A peace that is sought by meditation or other means of manipulating the thought processes, without reference to God, is a pagan peace. Also, trying to use God to gain peace of mind and health of body is a form of idolatry that is very prevalent and popular, but very shallow. This makes God the servant of man instead of man the servant of God.

The peace of God that "passeth all understanding" is not just something that we possess; it possesses us. It is a peace that will not break down but is available in the hour of crisis. In the midst of a stormy world, we can find a place of unshakable peace in the very heart of God. Our security is not in securities, but it comes from being secure in the God who changes not.

The deeper the stream of peace runs, the smoother the surface, even though at times the surface may appear disturbed. The Spirit makes it possible to experience peace even in the subconscious part of our being. It is difficult to know all the hidden motivations and inclinations of our human nature; but if we are fully surrendered to the Holy Spirit, He will cleanse and coordinate both the conscious and the subconscious into a peaceful calm. This is suggested in Philippians 4:7, which says His peace will keep our *hearts* (subconscious) and *minds* (conscious) through Christ Jesus.

Peace is not an attainment; it is an obtainment. Many people try to gain peace by their own blood and struggles and sacrifice. But it is not our blood that obtains peace; it is the precious blood of Jesus. Struggle and strife will only exhaust our peace; pride and selfishness will bring chaos;

but God will bring harmony as His peace reigns in our spirits and souls. Harmony within will produce harmony without.

"If it be possible, as much as lieth in you, live peaceably with all men" (Romans 12:18). We may not always be able to live peaceably with everyone, because the fault may lie in the other person. But as far as it depends on us, there must be peace between us and others. If there is discord, let us see whether it is our fault in any way. Have we been Christlike in our attitudes and actions? Have we truly practiced "in honour preferring one another"?

The primary cause of outer unrest may be in our relationship not with others but with God. If we are out of harmony with God, it is certain that we will have no harmony with ourselves or anyone else. If we seem to be living at cross-purposes with people and our lives are unhappy and restless, let us seek out the thing that is causing the conflict and turn it over to God. Let us also discipline ourselves to think thoughts of peace. If we have a habit of thinking upon the untrue, the dishonest, the unjust, and the impure, the very disharmony of those things will invade our spirits and then peace will flee from us.

"Thou wilt keep him in perfect peace, whose mind is stayed on thee: because he trusteth in thee" (Isaiah 26:3). May God help us to experience peace, think peace, and breathe peace so that those whom we meet today can feel and see our peace in Jesus Christ.

Long-suffering

The next three graces are long-suffering, gentleness, and goodness. This trio begins with the passive and ends with the active; for long-suffering is the patient endurance of injuries inflicted by others, goodness is positive action for the benefit of others (not just a kindly disposition), and gentleness is something in between. The three together promote the general comfort and productivity of life, reducing the friction that enters into all our interaction with our fellow men.

There is a close relationship between peace and long-suffering. Long-suffering is peace in action. It is a sweet temper manifested by the peaceful, patient endurance of affliction that others bring upon us. We often think of temper as an uncontrolled disposition or an explosive outburst of anger. But everyone has a temper; some tempers are uncontrolled, and others are sanctified, restrained, and long-suffering. This latter is how we want to view the grace of long-suffering.

Someone has said that long-suffering is love stretched out. Christian love is so elastic and tough that it does not break down into bad temper. It maintains a good temper amid the changing flow of human events; hence one can be calm and peaceful even under great stress. One may ask, "Did Jesus' peaceful calmness not snap when He drove the merchants and moneychangers out of the temple?" No, He was grieved at the hardness of their hearts, at their insensibility to human need. This made His anger constructive rather than destructive.

Our natural temper is bad temper; it lashes out—not in a redemptive way—when the ego is wounded. A good temper burns with the steady fire of redemptive intention; a retaliatory temper simply burns you up. Is that not strange, when it was intended to burn up the other person? If we give someone a piece of our mind, we lose our own peace of mind in the process.

God has given man a temper that need not be perverted and bad; it can be sanctified and highly valuable. Without proper temper, man would be unsuited to do God's great work. We live in a world of difficulties and tensions without and within, which God uses to bring us to the proper consistency and durability. Some of these tempering influences are "hot" (such as fiery trials of our faith), and some are "cold" (such as indifference or rejection from others). The degree of hardness and resiliency that we develop will depend on our response to such things.

Jesus had trials and tensions in His life on earth, but His tensions were harnessed to redemption rather than to anxiety and self-interest. He was on the way to the cross; and instead of becoming frustrated and bad-tempered, He allowed the tension to make Him calm and composed, with a prayer of forgiveness upon His lips. The tension was not released until He said, "It is finished." His experience on the cross drove Him not to pieces but to peace—the peace of achievement and victory.

Some people think they need to show bad temper to get things done for God. When Saul was anointed king, certain men despised him and brought no gifts. Saul could have used strong words and actions against them, for a good cause was at stake—"but he held his peace" (1 Samuel 10:27). A man's uncontrolled temper is never the means of achieving God's true goodness. "The wrath of man worketh not the righteousness of God" (James 1:20). We cannot use wrong means to accomplish right ends. Our tempers should be so tempered that they produce no tempests.

Some people seemingly must have the last word in every dispute, or they are not happy. It is good discipline for us to hold our peace and refrain from having the last word. Our last word in a controversy ought to be silence. Even if we have the last word, that often does not end the matter, for it usually precipitates a debate within us—between ourselves and our consciences. So really it is our consciences that have the last word.

To cultivate the grace of long-suffering, first get it fixed in your mind that bad temper is self-defeating—it gets you nowhere except backward. Exercise good temper, or long-suffering, as a life policy; it is not a luxury but a necessity. Remember that keeping your temper is a victory. A man always loses if he loses his temper, regardless of what temporary advantage he may gain. But if he controls his temper, he controls the situation.

When you are tempted to lose your temper, breathe a prayer for the other person as well as yourself. Remember, in that moment the center of the problem is not him but you. You are responsible for your actions and reactions. The first thing Jesus said to do if your brother wrongs you was, "Take heed to yourselves" (Luke 17:3). Trust in God for help in the hour of pressure, that you may act and react in a Christian way.

In addition, make a conscious decision not to be a touchy individual any longer. One person was so unaffected by criticism that someone said, "You don't even seem to know when you are insulted." This should be true of us all; we should be so long-suffering that we are the enemy of no man. One way to gain immunity against the criticism of others is to inoculate ourselves with mild doses of self-criticism. Then if someone points out a fault, we will be able to absorb the shock because we have dealt with similar criticism in our own meditations.

We need a memory that easily forgets the affronts of others. Some people have long memories for slights and hurts, and short memories for the blessings and good things of life. Do not take your hurts to bed with you, but pour them out to God and leave them there. If the memory keeps coming back, let the love of God invade you until there is no room for hurt feelings. Allow the sweet temper of Jesus to fill your heart and radiate from your countenance to the blessing of everyone you meet along the way.

Gentleness

"Put on therefore, as the elect of God, holy and beloved, bowels of mercies, kindness, humbleness of mind, meekness, longsuffering" (Colossians 3:12). The Greek word for *kindness* in the verse above is the same as the word for *gentleness* in Galatians 5:22. It is the noun form of the word for *kind* in the command, "Be ye kind" (Ephesians 4:32). So in considering the grace of gentleness, we are thinking essentially of kindness.

Without gentleness and kindness, there can be no virtue in any other virtue. Kindness puts a flavor into all the other virtues, without which they are insipid and unappealing. It is by no chance that this virtue is in the middle of the nine graces of spiritual fruit, for it flavors the whole. This is seen in the life of our Lord, not only in what He did but also in the spirit of His actions. The spirit of kindness is the benchmark of the Christian life, and without it no human can ever reach his highest potential in character and conduct.

The gentleness and kindness of our Lord is not mere sentimentalism; it can be very severe. He loves us so deeply that He often has to save us by hard refusals. His kindness can cut, but He always works redemptively, and His severity always brings healing security. He can be as hard as flint at one moment and as tender as a mother in the next. He can be tenderly terrible and terribly tender. God's unappealing acts of kindness are often the ones that stick best in our memories, while other acts of kindness are more easily forgotten and may have little impact on our lives.

Kindness pays, and it says what cannot be said in words. Just a simple smile may go further than a great deed. We need to exercise kindness not only for the benefit it brings to others but also for our own moral, spiritual, and physical well-being. Kindness and gentleness by their very nature involve reaching out, and we need this outgoing attitude to break the tyranny of self-preoccupation. Kindness is not an occasional deed or emotion; it is a life attitude, set in the will. "In her tongue is the law of kindness" (Proverbs 31:26). If we are unkind, we are spiritually sick, and it will possibly issue into physical sickness as well.

Nothing that we can do will compensate for a deficiency in kindness. Some people excuse themselves for a lack of kindness by referring to the many things they accomplish, but this does not suffice even for ministers and teachers who work long and hard. In 2 Corinthians 6:4–10, Paul named twenty-eight things by which he proved himself a minister of God, and in the center of those proofs he mentioned kindness. If kindness is not at the center, all the rest is sounding brass and a tinkling cymbal.

There are those who feel they are called of God to criticize people into doing better. We need to beware of such an attitude, for when we criticize someone, it tends to put him on the defensive. Then we need to find ways to justify our criticism, and any kindness within us withers and dies. Let us kill the critical spirit before it kills the kindness in us. As we look back and consider the people who have influenced us most, we find that it was those who exercised kindness and gentleness toward us.

Gentleness is actually a sign of strength. People with spiritual strength and assurance, who know what they believe and why, can most easily stand up to voices that challenge their viewpoint and authority. They can be gentle because they, like God, are strong in loving and seeking to help others.

It is weakness of character that makes people exacting and inconsiderate of others. When you see someone who makes arbitrary demands, he is most likely a person who does not feel sure of his own position. A weak and insecure parent or teacher must use threats in an effort to obtain obedience. Insecure leaders in the world or even in the church may also try to rule with a high hand. But the strong arm of outward control and rigid rules will hold sway only until people can get out from under the control. God is strong enough and great enough to be gentle. Are we?

"Be gentle unto all men" (2 Timothy 2:24). Gentleness suggests a willingness to be wronged rather than revenging injuries received. It will not break the bruised reed or quench the smoking flax. Gentleness trembles when it holds the rod. If words of reproof must be spoken, they come from a grieved and troubled heart. Greater force may overcome lesser force, but finally it is love that conquers. May we heed the call of Jesus, "Learn of me; for I am meek and lowly in heart: and ye shall find rest unto your souls."

Goodness

Goodness as a fruit of the Spirit includes a sweet disposition, an affectionate friendliness, a kindness of purpose and manner, a generosity of spirit, a consideration for others, and a readiness to sacrifice one's own things for the good of others. It is a kindness that wins the confidence and esteem of all those among whom we live and work. Only by the Spirit of God can we experience true goodness; any goodness of man is vanity. "There is none that doeth good, no, not one" (Romans 3:12).

But we tend to be like the rich young ruler and ask, "Good Master, what good thing shall I do, that I may have eternal life?" (Matthew 19:16). We need to have the concept that Jesus expressed in His reply: "There is none good but one, that is, God." The young man apparently thought that he had some goodness, and that he could do the required good if only he was told what it was. Such a false opinion of ourselves must be given up, and our being good must be grounded in God rather than ourselves. One of the hardest things in the world is to renounce our own goodness.

It is right to ask the question, "How can I be good like Thee?" But it is vain to seek goodness apart from God.

The young man thought he could claim eternal life as a reward for his own goodness. Jesus told him there is none good but one—God alone. He demonstrated the young man's lack of goodness by telling him to sell all his possessions and give the money to the poor. The young man was unable to do that, because he was lacking that one essential thing, the spirit of love. This is true goodness.

Romans 2:4 says, "The goodness of God leadeth thee to repentance." What more potent influence than mercy and love could God use to prevail upon man? And what influence is so likely to make a person repent of a wrong done to another person, than the injured person's response of goodness? If a man hurts his neighbor by word or deed and the neighbor meets him with angry words, it will only make the offender more stubborn and hostile. But if the neighbor patiently bears his attacks and unkind words, he heaps coals of fire on the offender's head; and by goodness and kindness, he melts his hard heart. This is true goodness, as demonstrated by God to us and as wrought by His Spirit in our hearts.

"Or despisest thou the riches of his goodness and forbearance and longsuffering; not knowing that the goodness of God leadeth thee to repentance?" We would not like it to be said that we despise God's goodness. Yet we must admit that we do not think as much of God's goodness as we might! A large part of true spiritual goodness is to recognize God's abundant goodness to us. His holiness required a sacrifice for our sins, and His love provided that sacrifice, even though we were His enemies. Only God has goodness of that degree.

The man who truly knows himself will acknowledge

that there is no good thing within him. If he finds anything good, he immediately concludes that it did not spring from himself. It is only the very bad who think themselves very good. If we are disposed to gloat over the praise we receive for our good actions, it is strong evidence that those actions were good in name only. Truly good actions cannot be done by those who are out of touch with God.

"Let another man praise thee, and not thine own mouth; a stranger, and not thine own lips" (Proverbs 27:2). It is of utmost importance for us to realize that any feeling of self-commendation is far from being the voice of God within us. A certificate of merit given to oneself by oneself cannot be taken at a very high value. Even when it seems to be well deserved, it is likely to be perverted by selfish motives. A man is the worst judge of his own worth and character.

Even when we make the most fair and honest estimation that one can imagine, it is likely to be seriously wrong. The reason is that when a man tries to evaluate his own merits, his thoughts are turned inward; and that is not at all wholesome. For the less a man focuses on himself, and the more he focuses on others, the better it is for him.

"Not he that commendeth himself is approved, but whom the Lord commendeth" (2 Corinthians 10:18). The man who is always ready to assert himself usually has little real goodness to assert. True dignity and self-respect produce a modest view of oneself and reserve in speaking of oneself. Those who commend themselves in words are not likely to commend themselves in deeds. The esteem they have for themselves is often inversely proportionate to the esteem others have for them.

"The fruit of the Spirit is in all goodness and righteousness and truth" (Ephesians 5:9). May the goodness of God to us produce the fruit of goodness in us, that we may "be ready to every good work."

Faith

The last set of graces is faith, meekness, and temperance, which refer to the regulation of Christian life. Faith in this context should be regarded not as the means of our salvation but as a guiding principle for living. Thus faith, or fidelity, is the secret spring of that meekness which is an ornament of great price, and it provides the strength for self-control, as implied in temperance.

"Not purloining, but shewing all good fidelity; that they may adorn the doctrine of God our Saviour in all things" (Titus 2:10). Fidelity suggests being loyal to the faith. It is the characteristic of one who has a constant, steadfast, resolute, unwavering commitment to the principles taught by Jesus Christ. Such a person is faithful in carrying out his obligations and vows.

Christian faithfulness is built on the principle of love, whereas the world's basis for fidelity is a principle such as "Honesty is the best policy." This makes honesty, or fidelity, a demand of duty, rooted in mere willpower; whereas in the fruit of the Spirit, fidelity springs forth from divine love. Christian fidelity is not a straining to be good; it is a surrender to the unbounded love and goodness of God. The dedicated Christian makes an absolute surrender to an absolute love, in absolute purity, with absolute fidelity and absolute usefulness.

Jesus emphasized the importance of fidelity when He

said, "He that is faithful in that which is least is faithful also in much. . . . If therefore ye have not been faithful in the unrighteous mammon, who will commit to your trust the true riches?" (Luke 16:10, 11). It may seem strange that our faithfulness with money and possessions is an index of our fidelity in spiritual matters, but that is what Jesus said. It does not take *much* of a person to be a Christian; it takes *all* of a person—himself and his possessions. May we not fail the day-by-day tests involving little things, lest He take away our stewardship and give it to another.

Our real dispositions come out most clearly when our behavior is most spontaneous, unpremeditated, and free from observation. If you want to know whether a man is faithful, do not judge him as he appears on the open platform of public life, but see how he speaks and acts in private, beyond the eyes and ears of the world. One can easily raise an artificial standard of moral obligation and make a great display of having certain scruples of conscience. But a really conscientious man will be conscientious in all things at all times.

The ultimate test of an individual's character is this question: Is the person honest? Is there any circumstance under which he will lie? If there is, the rest of his character is unsound. At a certain airport, a woman made a long-distance call right after arriving on an incoming flight. She explained to her partner, "I made a person-to-person call to myself at home and, of course, was told that I wasn't there. That let my family know I had arrived safely, but I didn't have to pay for the long-distance call." She thought herself clever, but actually she had sold herself cheap. This woman lost her self-respect for a dollar or two. May our moral joints not creak with infidelity, for God made us for truth in the inner parts. No dishonesty is worth the price we will pay in inward conflict and unhappiness.

Let us fix in our hearts the truth that nobody gets away with anything, at any place or any time, if that thing is dishonest or untrue. "All liars shall have their part in the lake which burneth with fire and brimstone" (Revelation 21:8). Satan keeps repeating to every son of Adam the well-worn lie, "Ye shall not surely die." But something does die the moment we are dishonest; death begins eating at our hearts. Indeed, sin often brings its own consequences already in this life. If we practice dishonesty, we will be punished by sin for our sin.

Examine your life, and see where there may be loose ends, broken promises, half-truths in words and actions, pretense in doing this or that, and unfinished tasks. Set out to finish the incomplete, fulfill the half-done, and gather up the loose ends; and when you do so by God's grace, a sense of well-being will flood your soul. Do not live under the haunting tension of a careless, haphazard approach to life. Our life is a sacred stewardship in which our fidelity is being tested at every position where Providence has placed us. May we be faithful in all things, that He may commit to us the true and eternal riches.

Meekness

Meekness in the Scriptural sense is a grace closely linked with humility, and the exercise of it is first and chiefly toward God. It expresses the spirit of one who accepts His dealings without disputing or resisting. This meekness toward God has a similar character in relation to men. A meek person will patiently accept and endure the injuries and insults of others, without feeling a spirit of revenge. He will also accept and follow the teaching of the Word as interpreted by a Scriptural brotherhood under the guidance of the Holy Spirit. Christian meekness stands in contrast to that self-reliant, rash, impulsive, impetuous spirit of the carnal-minded.

Meekness is not weakness; it is rather an integral part of Christian living. As we face new situations and unfamiliar circumstances in life, we can adapt to them in a destructive or constructive manner. We can retreat into the past and rest on previous achievements. Or we can try to leap into the future and dream of what we will do someday. Or we can seek to escape from the pressing issues by retreating into an inner state of mind and living in a world of mysticism. None of these responses will get us anywhere. The best way to face a new and pressing issue is to meekly yet boldly take hold of the situation by God's grace and transform it into an opportunity for life on a higher level.

Some people adapt to their surroundings by succumbing to them. They fit in anywhere and do not stand for anything. This is not meekness; it truly is weakness, and those who adapt in this manner will perish morally and spiritually. If we don't do what we know, it won't be long until we don't know what to do. Certainly we need to be adaptable—flexible on issues that involve no moral standards—but adamant on matters of Bible truth. These two principles properly blended make a man strong yet meek.

We must have Spirit-directed insight to know when to

be adaptable and when to be adamant. Those who can adapt themselves to their surroundings while still keeping Bible principles alive will move forward as "more than conquerors." All others will fall by the way, deceived by their false sense of meekness.

We are living in a world with a changing intellectual scene. Many people are not able to adapt and try to use an armor of dogmatic assertion as a defense in this new climate. Although we have an unchanging God and an eternal Holy Word, we must be open to new applications that are based on right principles. We could withdraw into a self-satisfied narrow-mindedness, thinking we are exercising fidelity and meekness. But the result may well be spiritual hunger and leanness of soul, to the neglect of new opportunities possible through the "great door and effectual" that is open to us.

It is of vital importance to exercise meekness when we give instruction to another. If we try to teach with "bitter envying and strife" in our hearts, we lie against the truth (James 3:14). We may acquire a certain superficial wisdom, but it does not come from God; it comes from our lower nature and perhaps even from the devil. The teacher must first possess the meekness that corresponds with his message. He needs the wisdom from above, which is "first pure, then peaceable, gentle, and easy to be intreated, full of mercy and good fruits, without partiality, and without hypocrisy" (James 3:17).

If we seek to help a brother who has been overtaken in a fault, we must do it with no feeling of superiority, but remember that we ourselves are delivered from sin only by the grace of God. The spirit of meekness will cause us to enter into his burdens and conflicts with him, and thereby be a means of encouragement to him in his struggles. But if we go with an exalted spirit, we deceive ourselves and will prove ourselves totally incapable of helping our brother. We must learn to assess our own works by comparing them with the standard of truth rather than with our brother's failures. If we have an improper view of our own burdens and conflicts, we cannot adequately help our brother with his. In fact, it may be that our brother's faults are so outstanding to us because we see our own sins in his life.

Some people try to draw others into controversies about matters of truth and principle, which inevitably lead to strife. They do this in an effort to justify their sins or to confuse believers on their convictions about truth. We should not strive with such people but be gentle toward them, looking for any possible opening through which we may slip a grain of truth. In such a setting, we will gain much more by meekness than by forceful logic.

A meek and quiet spirit is truly an ornament of great price. May we daily sit at the feet of Jesus and learn "the meekness and gentleness of Christ."

Temperance

Temperance comes last in the list of graces because control of one's actions is the end of all the Christian life. Like the governor in machinery, temperance adds nothing to the power at work, but it equalizes the power so as to produce a uniform, balanced result. If we begin with temperance, we are the center, we are trying to control ourselves, and we will be anxious lest we slip out from beneath our own control. Then we start each day with the idea that we will keep ourselves from every sin this day. And every night we come back a failure, for how can an uncontrolled will control an uncontrolled self?

But if we begin with love as in Paul's description, the spring of action is love for Christ—someone outside ourselves. This new affection breaks the tyranny of self-love and releases our powers to glorify Him. As a result, we are not anxiously tied up with self-control, but we are under a control that is relaxed and unstained, therefore beautiful. "The love of Christ constraineth us" (2 Corinthians 5:14); or in a literal sense, Christ's love "narrows us to His way."

Paul wrote that if we want to obtain the incorruptible crown, we must keep our bodies under and bring them into subjection (see 1 Corinthians 9:25–27). In the unregenerate man, the soul and the spirit of man are slaves of his body. But in the Christian, the body is subject to the soul and spirit, with the soul through the spirit in subjection to the Holy Spirit. The appetites of the body are controlled through self-denial. There is a proper place for earthly enjoyments, but they are kept under careful restraint. We must not be controlled by pleasures from within or pressures from without but by a Presence from above.

The apostle Peter mentioned temperance as something to be added by those who are partakers of the divine nature (see 2 Peter 1:6). The union of virtue and knowledge will bring in temperance, which enables a man to govern his appetites. Without that self-control, there is no unity of purpose, for a tumult of physical desires is always seeking to lead us in a multitude of different directions. As we master those desires through Spirit-directed temperance, we learn patience (patient endurance). And he who controls his bodily appetites will learn to endure hardness.

The matter of conflicting loyalties can be a very difficult test in life. There is only one way to build true character, and that is to choose one cause and serve it wholeheartedly. This central loyalty will put other loyalties in a subordinate position. Then life as a whole is coordinated, since the priority of conflicting loyalties is predetermined. For us as Christians, the central cause is Christ and His church. We must seek those first, and then all other things will find their place.

The life of temperance is a life of freedom—not to do as we like but to do as we ought. The price of freedom always includes discipline and submission. We need to be disciplined in thought, word, and deed—and especially in thought. Our meditation today will be our action tomorrow and for many days afterward. For we become what we think in secret, whether good or ill. So make it a point never to hold anything in your mind that you do not want to hold within you permanently.

If you dramatize temptation in your imagination, you will gather "gasoline" for the devil's spark. For example, if you dally with lustful thoughts, that dallying will become a doing. What you hold in your mind passes inevitably into action, if you hold it there long enough. Within the marriage relationship, if your partner becomes the means of self-gratification instead of someone to be loved and respected, disintegration sets in. Let us take control of our thoughts, or they will take control of us, and life will be full of frustration instead of creative enjoyment.

The tongue is an accurate index as to whether we have self-control. Too many people speak on the spur of the moment. Normally there are three steps in speaking: impulse, consideration, and speech. One who lacks temperance will leave out the second step and jump from impulse to speech. But the disciplined person pauses in between to consider what he plans to say. How long you pause is directly related to the amount of self-control you have. Of course, you dare not pause too long lest it lead to indecision, but pause long enough to be sure that the thing you say is what you really want to say.

Perhaps you write a stinging letter in the heat of an impulse. Do not send it right away, but pray and sleep over it. The next morning when your passion has subsided, you will probably tear up the letter in remorse and shame. *Spur-of-the-moment* and *off-the-cuff* are accurate descriptions of many people's lives today. They have lived so long on the spur of the moment that it is hard not to jump from impulse directly to word or deed. May God give us wisdom to speak or keep silent as we should, for the tongue can have poison or power—but it must not have both. "Out of the same mouth proceedeth blessing and cursing. My brethren, these things ought not so to be" (James 3:10).

Another area in which we need temperance is work. Some people are like a horse that lies down in the harness and refuses to move, and other people are like a horse that runs away and breaks the harness and smashes things. Temperate living has a proper balance. Between lying down and running away, temperance finds a life that is constructive yet disciplined.

Work is one of the best of self-disciplines; for when we

give ourselves to work, it calls our attention away from ourselves and our problems. We are happiest when we are engaged in a task that is within our powers but makes severe demands on our powers. Many folks are sleepless and restless, for they have little or nothing to do to fulfill their creative urge. They may resort to self-indulgence in eating, resting, or working, but that leads to self-exhaustion. Only the man who knows self-control in every area of life will find true fulfillment.

Desires are the God-given forces of the personality and as such are good and right. Without desires, life would hold little meaning or value. But there are some desires that are never right to express, and the only way to get rid of them is to replace them with higher desires. If life is to rise to a higher level, we can raise it only through temperance and discipline.

May we give all diligence to add these graces to our character and grow in them moment by moment, day after day. Christian character is not the result of natural disposition, or good childhood training, or favorable circumstances. It is the sum total of the graces of Jesus Christ, wrought in one who is purged from his old sins and governed by the Holy Spirit. Continuing in these graces is the only assurance that we will never fall away from God, and the full experience of them is a foretaste of heaven to come.

CHAPTER 4

"Quench Not the Spirit"

"Quench not the Spirit" (1 Thessalonians 5:19). In this verse the Spirit is likened to a flame that may be extinguished. It is an apt comparison, for the Spirit acts upon the believer's nature like a fire—warming, purifying, refining. When there is no more conviction for sin or no uneasiness about it, and when active interest in the good dies out, we are on dangerous ground. The Spirit of God takes His departure, and we know it not. What a tragedy! An evil spirit is likely to come in and take possession, and the latter end is worse than that of never having known the Holy Spirit.

One way to quench the fire of the Spirit is by smothering it. Sin can quench the Spirit as water quenches fire. Or we can become so immersed in the cares of life, that little time or thought is left for spiritual matters. A fire can also be extinguished by putting a great quantity of dirt upon it. We can quench the Holy Spirit by indulging in carnal desires or by setting our minds on earthly things. It is a fearful thought that we have the awful power of quenching the Spirit, who is the very life of our spirits and souls.

Another way to quench the Spirit is simply by neglect, by withholding fuel and thereby letting the fire burn out.

If this happens to a believer, the Bible becomes a dry and unappealing Book, and prayer becomes an empty ritual. Such a person needs to stir diligently among the ashes and rekindle the lingering spark. If the power of the Spirit is to move us, we must be diligent to keep the fire of love and faith burning in our hearts. Then the Word of God will be alive with freshness and meaning.

The context shows that quenching the Spirit does not refer to a sinner's resistance against the conviction of the Holy Spirit. For the words immediately following, "Despise not prophesyings," indicate that it refers to the work of the Spirit in inspiring utterances to the church. Sinners may grieve the Holy Spirit to the extent that the Spirit will no longer strive with them. But sinners do not possess the Holy Spirit so as to quench Him. A spiritual fire cannot be quenched before it is first kindled in the heart.

"Quench not the Spirit. Despise not prophesyings." Together these verses suggest the possibility of quenching the Spirit as He seeks to work in the church. In the absolute sense, of course, we cannot keep the Spirit from working, for He will function and express Himself in whatever way He chooses. However, the Spirit may be repudiated; He will never override the will of mankind. As in the individual, so in the church: we must ever be sensitive to the voice of the Spirit lest we quench Him and hinder His work.

Quenching the Spirit is only one way to sin against Him. Other ways include grieving Him (see Ephesians 4:30), lying to Him (see Acts 5:3), doing despite to Him (see Hebrews 10:29), and blaspheming Him (see Luke 12:10)—which is called the unpardonable sin. It is a serious matter to reject the Spirit's working in any way. We simply cannot have the presence of the Spirit when we desire Him and then lay Him aside when we want to follow our own lusts and passions. God's Spirit will not dwell in a divided heart; He must have full control, or He will have no control at all.

The Holy Spirit is not watching for an opportunity to depart from us. He wants to dwell in our hearts continually, and He will rule if our wills are broken and contrite. May we pray with David, "Take not thy holy spirit from me." May we keep the fire burning on the altar day and night, voluntarily laying ourselves there as a living sacrifice. May the Spirit and the Word of God lay our lives open and expose every fault, weakness, and sin in our hearts. And may the fire of God's Spirit come down from heaven and purify and consume the sacrifice, that our spirits and souls and bodies may wholly belong to Him.

Part 2

The Soul of Man

We will now consider the second part of man—his soul—which contains the will, mind, and emotions. The soul is the central part of man's being; here is found his real personhood. Highest in authority is the will, followed by the mind and then the emotions. However, the whole structure may be reversed. The will may give in to the emotions, especially strong emotions, and give them full authority over the whole being.

Emotions are often the first point of appeal that Satan uses to tempt and destroy man. Having taken control of them, he moves into the mind and the will; then finally he takes control of man's spirit, defiling his conscience and all but closing his avenue of contact with God. It is highly important that we stop Satan at his first attack before he does this deadly work.

God works through the spirit of man to regenerate the soul, which then affects his body. It must be in this order. We can be regenerated in the will, mind, and emotions only as our spirits are renewed through God's grace and the sanctifying power of the Holy Spirit.

CHAPTER 5

The Will

God has given man a will for making choices and decisions. The will has the highest position and authority in the soul. Man is free to choose among various options, but he has no control over the consequences of his choices, and often he has no power to reverse his decisions. Man must simply accept the results of his choices and actions, whether good or evil.

Man's obedience or disobedience to God is an act of the will; it is not based on mere emotion. His obedience affects his relationship with God; therefore, the relationship is also a matter of the will rather than emotion. The will was made to be in submission to an authority higher than itself. It does not have absolute authority, neither is it able to establish its own standard of right and wrong. The will has no power within itself to rise above its present condition.

God created man with a will having unrestricted power to choose what was right and good. Man's will was not laden with sin, but it was free to exercise the highest possible intelligence in its decisions. Man could have exercised his will by eating from the tree of life, and then he would have continued living forever in a state of perfection. But he chose to eat from the forbidden tree. God did not place that tree in the Garden of Eden to tempt man to do wrong, but to test man's loyalty to God and to give him the privilege of obeying God of his own free will.

Did Adam and Eve gain more knowledge as Satan had said they would? Mark it well, no man has ever increased his knowledge of right and good by disobeying God's commands. We can receive true knowledge and liberty only through complete obedience to the will of God. True obedience does not just happen; it is a deliberate act of the will. The more we choose to obey God, the more we will want to obey Him; and the less we obey, the less we will want to obey.

It is of the nature of the will to choose and do freely whatever it desires; but after it has decided to disobey God, the will is unable to make itself do right. After Adam and Eve sinned, they could not go back and be innocent again, neither could they decide to follow God's will as they had done formerly. Their wills were liberated with respect to obeying Satan, but bound with respect to obeying God. Adam and Eve had no power to rise above their fallen state or to change their perverted wills. This condition has been passed to all their sons and daughters to this day.

Before the Fall, Adam obeyed God simply because God said so. Adam knew that the consequence of disobedience was death, even before he disobeyed. There was no need to have any experience with evil. But Satan proposed, "You must do evil before you can know evil and its consequences." (He uses the same argument today.) After Adam yielded, his conscience was defiled with evil and was no longer able to give him positive direction. Yet God used man's knowledge of evil to help him flee from sin and its terrible consequences.

After seeing the absolute sovereignty of God, who cannot be resisted or challenged, one might think that He would force His will upon the creation. Why does He not protect and honor His authority by simply making all creatures obey His will? God receives the highest glory when His creatures choose to obey Him of their own will. God has so ordained that neither He nor the devil can control man's course of life without first obtaining his consent, for man's will is free.

Clearly, it was by an act of the will that man fell into sin and corruption. By another act of the will, man must recognize his sinful, helpless condition and choose to be redeemed by the power of Jesus Christ. We experience full redemption only as we willingly lay down our own works and choose Christ's provisions for salvation and victory over sin.

What about the teaching that "when grace is offered, we may refuse it if we will; and if we will, we may receive it"? We must carefully compare this doctrine with the Scriptures. In one passage, Jesus said that "no man can come to me, except the Father which hath sent me draw him" (John 6:44). John also wrote that the sons of God are born "not of blood, nor of the will of the flesh, nor of the will of man, but of God" (John 1:13). By these Scriptures and others, we conclude that no one can decide that he will get right with God at a certain time. A person must first hear God's Spirit calling before he can come to true repentance.

It is totally impossible for man of his own will to release himself from the hold of Satan. He may desire to live a better life, but he has no power to rise above his own inclination to do evil. All his intentions, resolutions, and commitments can never change his carnal will or his standing before Almighty God. His only hope is the salvation offered by Jesus Christ.

Yet salvation does include the exercise of the will. "Whosoever will, let him take the water of life freely" (Revelation 22:17). We dare not make room for the idea that "I'll wait to get saved until God decides to save me." For He is calling today, and "To day if ye will hear his voice, harden not your hearts" (Hebrews 3:15). The Lord "will have all men to be saved" (1 Timothy 2:4); He is "not willing that any should perish, but that all should come to repentance" (2 Peter 3:9).

Repentance from sin is a deliberate act of the will. We cannot be forced to repent; otherwise repentance is not genuine. True repentance includes confessing and forsaking sin with a broken and contrite heart. It means we are finished with having our own way and are ready to submit our wills to God's will.

God does not simply want to subdue the will; He wants to transform it (see Romans 12:1, 2). An obedient, transformed will is quite different from a will that obeys only because it is a duty or command. A transformed will is in harmony with God's will, and it obeys because it delights to do so. If our wills are surrendered to God, we will cease to resist God's will and grace. We freely submit to God's will because we have found that it is the best way.

Of course, there is still something within us that seeks its own way, for the old nature dies hard. But with time we learn that there is joy in giving up our desire to rule, and we find that it becomes easier to let go and let God have His way in our lives. Any hesitancy or lack of commitment shows a rising of our own wills. We must pray often, "Not my will, but Thine, be done."

We must remember that however grand our goals and ideas may seem to us, they can never match God's ways and doings. Our own thoughts and actions can easily run counter to the purposes of the Holy Spirit. We may think it is time to run when God desires us to walk, or we may want to walk when God intends that we stand still and let Him work. One rule we need to establish for ourselves is to make no provision for self-will. Any deviation from this rule will take us away from God's perfect will and from the abundant life of walking in perfect harmony with God's will.

Paul wrote, "I am crucified with Christ: nevertheless I live; yet not I, but Christ liveth in me" (Galatians 2:20). Being crucified with Christ means a total surrender of our wills to Christ. We cease to live by our own sinful wills and let God control them instead—yet we still possess them. The closer and longer we walk with Christ, the easier it will be for us to distinguish between our own self-will and the voice of the Spirit. It is common for our own wills to voice themselves first when a matter comes before us; but if we are sensitive to the Spirit, He will correct the first suggestion and reveal a better way. In this way we can walk in the Spirit and be "more than conquerors" through Christ.

Obedience

We are living in a permissive age with a free-for-all, do-as-you-please attitude. "You do your thing, and I will do mine." Our age has lost its roots and a solid frame of reference in established absolutes. Obedience is considered optional, and disobedience is held forth as true liberty. But God established a principle in the Garden of Eden that the soul that disobeys will die. The eternal truth is that death is the consequence for disobedience to divinely established authority.

Do we have the authority to require obedience in our permissive age? We certainly do. Indeed, children are the happiest when they obey. When children misbehave, they are really telling their parents, "I wonder where the boundaries are and how firmly fixed they are. Please show me." We must answer these questions by precept and example, along with firm discipline when our children cross the boundaries. We confuse them if we fail to make the lines clear. Also, discipline for disobedience will give the child a sense of release from the guilt of his wrongdoing. His sense of innocence is restored when punishment is inflicted. But after a child becomes accustomed to carrying a guilty conscience, punishment has little or no effect.

Anyone in authority soon learns that there are two kinds of obedience. There is willing obedience, recognized by a happy smile on a child's face; and there is forced obedience, evident in the lagging of a child when he is told to do something. He often does little things along the way to show that in his heart he is not really obeying. With time, such an attitude will reach a climax. Either the child will see his error and learn true obedience, or his rebellion will continue until stopped by authoritative action.

True obedience is imperative in every godly home. A child who is well trained in obedience from infancy to twelve years of age will have a foundation for submission and obedience the rest of his life. Any deviation not only frustrates and confuses the child but also makes it practically impossible for parents to require obedience at a later time.

The standard of obedience can change in less than one generation. Disobedience makes inroads until parents finally remain silent to avoid confrontation with their children and youth. Proven principles in the home and church are cast aside, and compromise and concession are the rule of the day. Negotiated obedience and reluctant obedience are simply disobedience by other names. True obedience is prompt and not dallying. It may be accompanied by questions, but they dare not be designed to challenge authority or to delay obedience. A truly obedient child will honor the wishes of his parents, whether they are present or absent.

In a godly home, punishment is not a last resort that a defeated parent uses to vent his frustration. Rather, it is applied to correct the child when his carnal nature expresses itself. Parents show true love by administering proper discipline and restraint while the child is young, and the result is security and rest for the child. Examples of when a child should be punished include deliberate disobedience as well as lying, stealing, bad language, and displays of temper. The age and understanding of the child must be considered when discipline is applied. Firm discipline does not mean that children should be beaten or abused in any way.

Some parents will do anything to avoid a confrontation with their children. Once a child learns to manipulate his parents, he will play the game over and over until the parents are so frustrated that one of two things is likely to happen. The parents may throw up their hands in despair and let the school system or the state take control of the child, or they may become so enraged that they abuse the child. Children need discipline, but it should be given in love and not in anger and heated emotion. Such an approach only infuriates the child and never corrects the problem.

Although children's responsibility to their parents changes as they reach adulthood, the duty of respect never changes. Respect for parents is a responsibility that continues throughout life. Grown children ought to spend time reflecting on the benefits they received from their parents, rather than criticizing their mistakes. If we as parents fail to respect our own parents, we are poorly equipped to teach our children the respect they need to learn. But if we walk in the way of godliness and teach it to our children, that is the greatest honor we can give to our parents.

Love makes obedience easy and duty delightful. "If ye love me, keep my commandments" (John 14:15). Obedience is the true test of love.

A Submissive Will

What is a submissive will? It is not determined by how much we submit to or how many things we give up. We may submit to a host of unpleasant things and still not have a submissive will. Neither is it a matter of being

The Will

satisfied only when we get what we want. A submissive will goes beyond our present circumstances and even beyond the question of who is in authority. In fact, a submissive will is totally beyond our natural ability to obtain.

By nature, man is stubborn and rebellious and unyielding. He does not submit without resistance, nor does he willingly yield to the control of another. This obviously applies to those who are unsaved, but by no means does self-will end as soon as we come to Christ for salvation. The conversion experience is only the starting point.

God's work of regeneration is aimed primarily at our wills; it is here that the greatest work of salvation is done. The reason is that all the rest of man's being—spirit, soul, and body—is subservient to the will. Even the spirit of man must yield to the rule of the will. This yielding of our wills to God's will is instantaneous at our new birth, but it is also a lifelong process. For we may be united with Christ in our minds and emotions while still not being united with Him in will. A truly submissive will involves such a union.

Our perfect example is Jesus, who submitted His will to the Father's will. He lived in perfect union with His Father and always did those things that pleased His Father. When facing the cross, He resigned His will: "Not my will, but thine, be done." Jesus' submission came as a specific act of His will. He could have willed otherwise if He had yielded to Satan.

God is not satisfied until our wills are completely united with His. To produce this end, He may permit many experiences to come into our lives—some desirable and some not so desirable. He may let us bow our heads in pain until

He touches our wills through this form of discipline. He may allow us to lose health, reputation, position, and even our usefulness, to bring us into conformity with His will. God may strip us of everything we hold dear, including our closest friends, and may even deprive us of the joyous sense of His presence (as Job experienced). God will use whatever it takes to show us that He saved us not for our own personal enjoyment but for His will and glory.

Our submission should not be that of a servant who follows his master's orders, but that of a son who knows his father's heart, whose will is one with his father's, and who delights to do his father's will because of the love that they share. Yet there lies within our wills a constant tendency to seek our own way when opportunity affords. We may conform to God's will on most occasions, but at times there is a mighty struggle between our wills and God's will. Then we must look to God for grace to yield, knowing that He loves us perfectly and that His will is for our ultimate good.

What are some reasons that submission is difficult? One is the present age of luxury and indulgence, which fosters a forward, aggressive spirit that militates against submission and obedience. As we become more successful, we become less dependent on the help and counsel of others and, therefore, less submissive to one another. Our prosperity even makes us feel less dependent on God, with the result that submission to Him becomes less important, in our estimation.

Along with a prosperous age—strange as it seems—there comes a state of insecurity and unsettledness, which in turn brings more rebellion and disobedience. This uneasiness is manifest not only in the world but also in the church. People become dissatisfied with things in general and with the church in particular: its principles, applications, and leaders. Many churches make changes in an effort to accommodate the people, but they only help them along in their dissatisfaction and rebellion.

The only solution is genuine repentance and willing submission; no church can operate effectively in any other way. A carnal, worldly congregation will soon become segmented, with people pulling in different directions. It should be obvious that people who have learned to submit to each other can get along better than people who insist on having their own way.

Let us sincerely repent of any insubmission to our Lord and save ourselves the misery of living in halfhearted commitment. Jesus gave up everything He had—including His life—so that we might be delivered from our old self-will and might experience a calm, restful triumph in Him.

A Passive Will

There is a fine line between a will fully surrendered to God and a passive will; yet there is a line and a difference. A passive will is one that has ceased to be active in ruling the spirit, soul, and body. It offers no opposition or resistance in the decisions and choices it does make. It is empty and useless, silent and irresponsible, unwilling to be held accountable.

A passive will manifests itself in various ways. For example, we have mouths but we refuse to talk. We know we should say something, but we remain silent. Perhaps we imagine that if the Holy Spirit inspired us with a profound message, we would speak out with zeal and boldness. We do need the Holy Spirit to direct our speech, but He will not compel us to speak if we have no interest in doing so. There may be a similar passivity about using our hands or feet for the work of Christ. We refuse to exercise our wills and simply wait for God to move us, thinking this is being fully surrendered to God.

Spiritual discernment is needed here. We must not let our wills exert themselves against God's will, yet we must use our transformed wills to fulfill His will. Have you ever seen a person who claimed to be fully surrendered to God but never seemed to grow in his Christian life? He is satisfied to let others think for him, and he readily agrees to almost anything. If someone asks what he thinks about a certain matter, he says, "Whatever you decide is fine with me." But after others make a decision on it, he is not satisfied and says, "That is not the way I would have decided." Even worse, he may be offended because he was not included in the decision and may withdraw deeper into passivity.

The enemy of our souls will use a passive will to his greatest advantage. He does not mind if we outwardly submit to God and the church, if our submission grows out of a passive will. "I'll just do as I'm told and ask no questions." This may sound right, but underneath there may be a spirit of rebellion or even plain laziness. To simply obey without understanding the principles involved will not stand up under testing. Such passive obedience may be suitable for new believers but not for those who should be mature in the Christian faith.

The Will

A believer who waits for some external force or strong emotional drive before he moves forward will often lose the opportunity to make decisions. While he waits, someone else decides for him; and finally it is hard for him to make even the smallest decisions. Passive thinking produces a passive faith, and passive faith leads to committing many sins of omission. Not doing what we ought is just as sinful as doing what we ought not. Eventually a passive faith leads to apostasy and worldliness. Even when we know what we should do and want to do it, we will be unable to act for fear of making a wrong move.

God never imposes His will on man's will. He gave man a free will, and He wants man to use it actively and consciously in doing His will. God transforms the will of the believer so that he can choose God's will, but the believer is always responsible for what he decides. Man chooses his eternal destiny by choosing or rejecting the will of God.

A person with a passive will may think, "Someday I will choose to stop sinning and call upon God for forgiveness. Sometime I will live a better life, but not now. If I turn to God today, I'm afraid I won't hold out; and if I can't hold out, it would be better if I had never started." This is all passive thinking, and it gives the will one more opportunity not to decide. Each time we take such a course, we weaken our wills to make a positive decision later. Actually, we strengthen our wills in a negative direction; for in choosing not to decide, we are making a choice.

A passive will may also manifest itself in so-called meekness and humility. True, meekness and humility are an essential part of the believer's experience; there can be no Christian life without them. But to look down on ourselves because we feel incapable of certain responsibilities or inferior to certain people is not true meekness or humility. It is rather weakness in our inner beings that results from our fear of making decisions that may prove wrong. Joshua made the decisive statement, "As for me and my house, we will serve the LORD" (Joshua 24:15). May God give us grace to take a similar stand for His glory.

Inner Conflict and Indecision

To be at our best, there must be no division or conflict within our souls. Jesus said, "If a house be divided against itself, that house cannot stand" (Mark 3:25). It is the nature of reality that inward division brings inward disintegration. The nerves and the body in general can stand almost anything, provided there is inner harmony. And there is only one thing that makes people well who have inner conflict: a release from that conflict. Some people are full of inner confusion, and this confusion spreads sickness through the mind and body. Often they seek treatment for physical symptoms when the disease itself is rooted in the soul.

Thinking is not tiresome; it is conflict in thinking that consumes one's energies and produces weariness. Harmonious thinking is creative and recreative; it leaves one with a sense of being built up. Christianity introduces a new standard into one's life; but if this new life is allowed only a partial functioning, it will produce conflict in one's mind and soul. Many people have just enough Christianity to make them miserable. They are not free to act according to the standard of the world, neither are they free to do what the Christian way demands. As a result, their religion creates

THE WILL

irritation instead of beauty and harmony.

Some people put forth great effort to live a Christian life. They toil with all their might to eradicate their faults and wring out the last drop of self. The battle is such that a civil war rages right within their souls. In a sense, they are like the man who lived among the tombs, not that they are afflicted with evil spirits but that they are tormented by a multitude of voices. If one experiences conflicting voices within himself, he is headed for a dwelling among the tombs, far from the place of peace and harmony. United within, we can endure almost anything without; but divided within, the smallest circumstance can take us down.

We must have a single-minded devotion that holds us together, or we will fall to pieces. Jesus said, "The light of the body is the eye: if therefore thine eye be single, thy whole body shall be full of light. But if thine eye be evil [double], thy whole body shall be full of darkness. If therefore the light that is in thee be darkness, how great is that darkness!" (Matthew 6:22, 23). Inner division will have its effect on all our ways and make us unstable and ineffective. "A double minded man is unstable in all his ways" (James 1:8).

Inner division has serious consequences for all people, whether saints or sinners. No one can long afford to hold conflict within himself; it must be resolved. Personal achievement is impossible save where the motives of life are working in harmony. Contentment is not attainable unless one has a single set of desires to govern his activities. This is illustrated by the man who is not sure of his aim in life and knows not what he wants to do or be. The only real solution is to surrender everything to Christ, including all our conflicts and confusions, and find in Him true peace and purpose in life.

A subtle form of inner conflict is indecision, which leads to uncertainty and procrastination. There is a saying that procrastination is the thief of time. It is even worse than that; procrastination is the thief of character. We need to correct our tendency to shy away from dealing with unpleasant things. For putting things off does not make them any more pleasant, and it contributes to weakness of character.

Some people's indecision is such that they seem to throw their minds into neutral and go wherever they are pushed. This may be one way to get along with others, but it will gain us little appreciation because people respect a man who can make most of his own decisions. Then there are those who make tentative decisions but are never sure about them. They go over and over their decisions, constantly worrying over whether they are right and wondering if they should have decided otherwise. This kind of indecision is pure misery.

We must learn to make decisive choices in order to develop true character. To do this, simply bring the matter into the light of God's presence and Word, and make a decision according to the best of your understanding; then leave it there. Often it is not so important *what* we decide as *that* we decide. We need to make each decision with faith in God and calmness of heart and then leave the matter decided—trusting that God will show us in good time if we should choose differently.

Do not decide matters necessarily on the basis of a

predicted result, but on the basis of principles. If you are always trying to foresee the results of an action, you will always be in a state of doubt. The most important question is not "How will this decision affect me?" but rather "What is the right thing to do regardless of how it affects me?" The results can never be bad if we always try to do what is morally right.

There may be occasions when we need to reverse ourselves in a decision, but even this we can do with composure. God can overrule wrong decisions honestly made, and He can still make things work together for good. A reversal from a wrong decision is the only road to a right decision. If Christ rules in our hearts, He will help us with our decisions, and we will be "more than conquerors" over indecision and inner conflict.

Always Being Right

One of the most important lessons in life is to learn that we do not have to be always right. There is great virtue in being able to say, "I'm sorry; I was wrong." Only proud men are always defending themselves and trying to prove themselves right. Humble men feel a central rightness and can put up with marginal mistakes, but to hold the line at every marginal issue is only to reveal our smallness. So if one thinks he must be always right, he becomes always wrong. The more perfect a man is, the more he can put up with imperfections in others. Jesus was so perfect that He could endure the worst of imperfections in people.

There are people who, if they just once said, "I was wrong," would be different people. Nothing is more beautiful than the tear of repentance on the face of a penitent one. For that teardrop opens the resources of grace and floods the soul with pardon and reconciliation. If we live by defense, we live by fear. But if we have nothing to defend, we live by faith and we melt the defenses of other people.

We do need to make a sincere effort to do right, according to the best light we have. But if we fail, Jesus is standing ready to take care of our mistakes and sins. Mistakes honestly made do not break our fellowship with Christ or each other; for if we walk in the light as He is in the light, we experience continuous cleansing through His blood. But we must acknowledge our wrongs.

So we do not have to be always right. We may blunder and stumble; but if we do, let us fall on our knees in humble confession. Then let us get up again with renewed strength and direction, and profit from the mistake. This is not a license for a careless attitude, defeated living, or a sub-Christian experience. If we refuse to walk in the light as we see it in Jesus, the light ceases. But if His light shows that we have done wrong, let us be willing to acknowledge it and seek His cleansing. God's all-seeing eye is not looking for our weaknesses and blunders, but for our right attitude about them.

"For I say, through the grace given unto me, to every man that is among you, not to think of himself more highly than he ought to think; but to think soberly, according as God hath dealt to every man the measure of faith" (Romans 12:3). It is a besetting temptation of the human nature to think too highly of oneself. Man is prone to exaggerate his own abilities and to minimize his faults, while belittling the abilities of his neighbor and magnifying his failures.

The Will

We need the grace of God to have a proper and modest view of ourselves.

It would be good for us to pray, "Lord, when we are wrong, make us willing to change. When we are right, make us easy to live with. And even when we know we are right, make us willing to be accused of being wrong." We need to work harder at being what we should be than at hiding what we are. We may be wrong many times, but we are not a failure until we refuse to acknowledge it.

When we are right, many will not remember; and when we are wrong, many will not forget. A man should never be ashamed to admit that he was wrong, for it is but another way of saying that he is wiser today than yesterday. Most men learn from their own mistakes, wise men learn from the mistakes of others, but fools never learn from either. "Seest thou a man wise in his own conceit? there is more hope of a fool than of him" (Proverbs 26:12).

Let it be established that always being right includes admitting when we are wrong. Such an admission actually builds respect rather than weakening it. We should never think for one moment that we gain people's esteem by covering our wrongs. They know them anyway; so if we cover wrongdoing because of our status or reputation, our wrong only increases.

When our wills are lost in God's will, we can be accused of wrong even though we are right, and we can be right even though we do not have the last word. We do not need to prove that we are right, for truth and right will stand on their own. Regardless of how right we may be, we need the humility to say, "By the grace of God I am what I am."

"More Than Conquerors"

Our Native Desire

When God created man, He placed within him a desire to go forward, to be creative, to gain more than he had. Although man's needs were fully supplied and he experienced a great measure of satisfaction in Eden, there was still a drive for progress. Animals are propelled by instinct, and plants respond to the stimuli in their environment. But man is motivated by an innate desire placed within his soul and directly associated with his will. What is it that makes a baby want to turn himself over, to crawl, to walk and talk? It is this natural, inborn desire.

Satan took advantage of man's native desire when he tempted Adam and Eve. He made the forbidden tree look good for food, pleasant to the eyes, and desirable to make one wise. When Adam and Eve ate the fruit, their eyes were opened to evil—the very thing God did not want them to see and desire. Ever since, man's native desire has been corrupted by sin. Instead of being consistently beneficial, man's desire tends to destroy himself as he seeks ways to fulfill the appetites of his flesh. And as with the children of Israel in the wilderness, God allows man to have what he wants, but to his own hurt.

With the native desire unchecked, man becomes essentially a self-serving creature. He becomes preoccupied with self-glory, self-exaltation, self-love, and self-importance. He finds his chief delight in doing what he wants. He aspires to a lofty position so that he may be honored before men. He uses every effort and means to push himself to the front. He takes pride in his position, family, ability, and good management. He feels self-content as he compares himself with those who cannot attain to his status.

When he is not fully accepted for his efforts, he suffers a deep wound. But if his peers admire him and praise him, his heart is overjoyed. He considers the praise of others to be his rightful due. If he is not elevated as he desires, he has no scruples about belittling others to make himself look better. All this and more is characteristic of unregenerate men and women. But sad to say, the same self-centered drive is also present in the lives of many professing Christians.

The quest for growth and depth in the Christian experience is common among believers. But if we trace our desires back to their true source, we may be surprised to discover that they are rooted in a basic self-centeredness. So reckless is our selfish drive that we will use even this means to satisfy ourselves and impress others. We pretend to be seeking growth and maturity when all the while we are very immature in our undertakings. Sometimes we regret our pretense, but for the moment it makes us feel great and tall. Our natural desires cause us to maneuver for even a little ground to stand upon—all in the name of seeking a deeper life in Christ.

Our quest for Christian growth and depth can be used by God only as we allow Him to sanctify us wholly in spirit, soul, and body. The crucifixion of our native desires may be one of the most painful things in our Christian experience, but it must be done. However, we may be so bent on satisfying the fondness of our flesh that we are blind to the true nature of our pursuits. Even in spiritual matters, we may make decisions for our own benefit and pleasure rather than for the glory of God and the benefit of others. Those who love pleasure more than principle will soon lose both.

"More Than Conquerors"

We need to be sanctified by God's regenerating Spirit so that our pursuit of holiness and our performance of good deeds will be a true benefit to God's kingdom. In this way we can be "more than conquerors" even in the deepest desires of our hearts.

Our Affections

God wants the total affection of our hearts. In His wonderful, fatherly love, He ardently seeks the affection of His children. We have little trouble with giving Him our time, money, or countless other things, but to give Him our perfect love we find most difficult. Jesus reaffirmed the command, "Thou shalt love the Lord thy God with all thy heart, and with all thy soul, and with all thy mind" (Matthew 22:37). This means that God is to be loved with all our powers and faculties, and that nothing is to be preferred above Him.

God deserves our love because He is supremely good and glorious. There is no other object so worthy of our hearts' full devotion. Our love to God is a reflection of God's love to us; it is our hearts' response to His goodness and kindness. He revealed Himself even when we were most unloving, so that we might love Him supremely. "But God commendeth his love toward us, in that, while we were yet sinners, Christ died for us" (Romans 5:8).

The intense love of God toward His children should draw from them a sweet, compelling obedience to all His commandments. Yet His first interest is not our laboring for Him but our loving Him. How strong is our love for God? Is it tainted with a secret affection for this world? Nothing satisfies God's heart as does our love, and nothing but

God's love can satisfy the longing of our hearts. Friends, family, and things will leave our hearts empty if God's abiding love is absent.

One way we can discern the quality of our love is by its results. Do the world's attractions have a strong appeal to us, or have they lost their glitter in the glorious light of God's love? We cannot love God and the world at the same time. What about those long periods of trial that test our faith? Can we continue loving God even when He seems to have forsaken us? The Lord sometimes allows these painful experiences as a way to wean us from a selfish love toward Him for the benefits we receive. He wants us to have an unrelenting love that says, "Although the fig tree shall not blossom, neither shall fruit be in the vines; . . . the flock shall be cut off from the fold, and there shall be no herd in the stalls: yet I will rejoice in the LORD, I will joy in the God of my salvation" (Habakkuk 3:17, 18).

Our emotions must be in subjection to our wills, which in turn must be governed by God's Spirit through our spirits. Let emotion rule, and the believer will go to pieces in adverse circumstances. But let the Holy Spirit rule through a submitted will, and the believer can handle anything by God's grace. Love for God includes strong impulses of emotion when we first receive salvation, but it must move away from that to a settled and fixed act of the will.

Satan tries to overcome God's children by confusing them in their affections. One tactic is to have the believer relax and depend on pleasant emotions and sensational feelings. Another is to put love for other people in competition with love for God. Nothing stirs our affections as family and friends do. But human affections must always be subordinate to our affection toward our heavenly Father. No human love can give the satisfaction that God's love provides for the soul. Many fail here as they seek from man what can be found only in God. The moment a Christian pursues a love outside of God, his spiritual life begins to decline.

This is not to suggest that we neglect love for others, because the Bible repeatedly admonishes us to love our brethren and even our enemies. But no human love is to transcend our love to God. He is a jealous God who will not share His love or allegiance with another. He seeks (and deserves) first place in all things.

God wants us to love others for His own sake, not for the benefit we may receive. So when He tells us to love certain ones, we will love them regardless of how unloving they are or how they mistreat us. And when He directs us to end a relationship with someone for His sake, we can do that too. This is the way of the cross. Only as we submit to its power will we be rid of our self-centered love to God and others.

Sometimes God breaks the ties of human love to show us how attached we have become in our affections for other people. He may remove a spouse, a child, or a friend by death or perhaps by calling the person to serve in a faraway place. Of those persons or things we hold dear, He may say, "They are mine." He may also remove worldly securities on which we have come to depend. If our hearts are fully consecrated to God, He can deprive us of our dearest friends or possessions and we will still love Him.

Even when our affections are focused on God, they must be entirely under the Spirit's direction. A man can talk about his great love for God and even shed some tears when speaking about the Lord's suffering and death. In so doing, he may experience an unspeakable, burning affection for the Lord Jesus and conclude that such a feeling surely comes from God. But this affection comes and goes with the emotion of the moment, and it serves only to make the individual feel good. It is not an abiding love that comes from the Spirit of God, and it does not affect his life.

The natural man may love God and others to some degree, but he loves himself first and above all. He esteems his interests more important than those of God and others; therefore, he can never fully sympathize with the needs and desires of others. The focus of our love must change from self to God and others so that we can share their joys and sorrows, help to bear their burdens, and give ourselves in service to them. No longer do we love ourselves primarily, but we love those whom God loves. No longer do we count ourselves better than others, but we have the same regard for them as for ourselves. We can even sacrifice what we need so that others can have what they need. This is the kind of love that moved God to provide redemption for sinful man, and it is the love of the saints who are overcomers through Christ.

Faith

"Now faith is the substance of things hoped for, the evidence of things not seen" (Hebrews 11:1). Christian faith is an act of the will of man in believing in God and His eternal absolutes. It is higher than reason, yet the two are not entirely in opposition. For many truths of

God's revelation are reasonable, but it takes faith to apprehend them. Faith is far more than the assent of the reason and more than an act of the mind. It is a gift that God gives man so that he can believe in the eternal God, who is a Spirit and cannot be perceived by the physical senses.

Faith is the eye of the soul that looks into the realm of spiritual realities. Its telescope is the Bible, without which man could never see beyond the natural sight of reason. Faith is also the hand of the soul that grasps the promises of God. Faith lays hold on the invisible realities—the unseen, yet real and absolute. And faith is an anchor fastened to the eternal, unchanging Rock, who is God the Father and Jesus Christ our Saviour.

"So then faith cometh by hearing, and hearing by the word of God" (Romans 10:17). We must know before we can believe, yet we must believe before we can know. If we have knowledge without faith, we can do no more than the devils, who believe and tremble. But as believers, we have access to truth, by exercising faith, that transcends the logical processes of reasoning.

God has also chosen to reveal spiritual truths through the five senses. Scores of people in past ages have seen with their own eyes and heard with their own ears many clear demonstrations of these truths. Though we may not have similar experiences, we need to exercise faith in the testimonies of these people. Hebrews 11 is an ample catalog of such human testimonies. The faithful brethren of the present and the more recent past are additional witnesses to divine truth. Together, the record of the written Scriptures, the testimony of faithful brethren, and the revelation of God's Spirit through our intuitions provide an unshakable foundation for our faith.

Though faith is of prime importance, we also need a certain amount of reason to justly recognize and weigh the evidences of God's revelation. We need reason to comprehend that Jesus Christ did fulfill the Messianic prophecies of the Old Testament. We need reason to understand and accept the claims of God upon our lives. We need reason to let God work regeneration in our souls, and we need reason to work out the daily details of the overcoming life.

By faith we receive not only salvation but also assurance of salvation. We can be sure about the forgiveness of our sins, the indwelling of the Holy Spirit, the love and mercy of God, and the eternal glories of heaven. All this lies within the scope of our faith. Moreover, faith is like a telephone cable that carries thousands of messages between ourselves and our Father. Through the gift of prayer and faith, we can have inexhaustible and unlimited communication with the unseen God in heaven.

In the body, we live by what we see, hear, handle, taste, and smell. But in the soul, we live by faith in things we cannot perceive with the physical senses. We live by faith as we walk with God. This life of faith cannot be separated from a life of holiness, for a holy God will not walk with an unholy person.

There is much we cannot explain. We are not told that we must understand, but only that we must believe. In fact, true faith has a childlike simplicity, which follows God without questioning. Faith enables us to stand for what we do not understand. To those who believe, no explanation is necessary. "God said it; I believe it; that settles it."

Faith is wrought by the Holy Spirit, beginning with the first stirring of conviction and growing into a full confidence in Christ. Some like to argue which comes first: repentance or faith. The two are so interrelated and interdependent that it is hard to conceive of having one without the other. Faith begins in repentance and continues to the appropriating of Christian grace, which can be received only by a contrite heart. If there is no repentance, no longing for deliverance from sin, no brokenness or conviction for sin, there can be no real faith.

God gives the facilities of faith—the powers of the will and the mind—to be employed in hearing and believing God's Word. He awakens in the soul the sense of guilt necessary for starting on the course of repentance to salvation. But God will not override the will so that it is compelled to choose His grace and salvation. If He did that, man's free choice would be violated and there would be no place for faith in believing. Neither could God rightly condemn man for rejecting Christ or reward him for receiving Christ.

We are saved by faith, justified by faith, and adopted as God's children by faith. We walk by faith, live by faith, and overcome the world by faith. At His second appearing, Christ Jesus will not forget our "work of faith" or "the patience and the faith of the saints." Then we shall see Him face to face, and we shall know even as also we are known.

CHAPTER 6

The Mind

The human mind is a subject so complex that even the most intelligent person cannot explain its workings. The Scriptures have much to say about the mind as well as the heart. It seems that the mind is the faculty of conscious thought, and the heart is the faculty of subconscious mental activity. Memories and impressions are stored in the heart to be called up into the conscious mind. This is why the Bible says, "Keep thy heart with all diligence; for out of it are the issues of life" (Proverbs 4:23).

Much activity of our minds takes place subconsciously, beneath the surface of our awareness. For example, we may try in vain to recall what a certain person's name is or where we put a certain thing. Finally we give up and go on our way—and later the desired memory suddenly comes to mind. What happened is that the subconscious mind continued to work on the problem, even though the conscious mind had dismissed it. Then when the answer was found, the subconscious mind presented it to the conscious mind.

God made the human mind to think, perceive, reason, and remember in relation to what it knows and understands. Man's mind was created pure and apparently with vast powers that have been unknown since the Fall, as illustrated by Adam's naming of the animals. But when sin entered, man's mind became a battlefield where Satan and his forces contend for evil against the holiness and righteousness of God. Christians are also active in this warfare, which includes "pulling down of strong holds" and "bringing into captivity every thought [or mind] to the obedience of Christ" (2 Corinthians 10:4, 5).

Every temptation that comes to man is presented to his mind. Satan works through the five senses of man's body to arouse an unlawful desire. He injects a thought corresponding to that desire; and if the will decides to yield, Satan uses the mind again to activate the body in committing the sin. Thus Satan's control of the unregenerate mind is inseparable from his control of the body. Each serves the other, and both are under the dominion of Satan.

When man comes to a saving knowledge of Christ, he experiences a transformation of his heart and mind that sets him apart from the mentality of this world (see Romans 12:2). He offers the members of his body as "instruments of righteousness" to do the will of God, with the result that temptations no longer have a foundation to build upon as they did formerly. Temptations look different to the believer because their appeal is now overshadowed by the knowledge that yielding brings defeat and misery.

But Satan and the flesh do not give up easily. We must constantly guard against the idle thoughts that would pervade our minds, for Satan will surely use them to his advantage. We must diligently exercise our minds to think on things that are true, honest, just, pure, and lovely, as Paul instructed in Philippians 4:8.

Some professing Christians are so broad-minded that they give ear to any and all voices, even taking pride in their tolerant attitude. Others become so narrow-minded that they are full of prejudice and have already decided what is truth and what truth they will accept. They tend to reject plain truth while claiming to defend the truth. Both kinds of individuals may boast of how spiritual or how conscientious they are, but all the while they give abundant evidence of an unrenewed mind. We need to beware of thinking we have God's thoughts when they are only notions of our own contrivance.

Both the Holy Spirit and evil spirits can put ideas into our minds. How can we tell the difference between the two? First, any revelation, vision, or special impression that transcends the normal working of the mind (such as a hallucination) is not of God. A leading of the Holy Spirit always comes when the believer's mind is operating normally, for that is the only way God works.

Second, all that comes from God will be in harmony with His character and with the Scriptures. But the suggestions of Satan correspond to his character and appeal to the base desires of our flesh. If one follows the moving of evil spirits, he may actually come under strong passions that cause him to lose control of his body and mind.

God is persuasive yet gentle; He does not try to force a man against his own will. The Holy Spirit never prevails upon a man to take action immediately. He gives man time to think, consider, and investigate. But Satan operates without consent. He seeks to confuse and paralyze man's mind so that he cannot think intelligently or reason soundly. In this way, the devil tries to coerce man into doing what he wants.

We need to be renewed in the spirit of our minds. "Let this mind be in you, which was also in Christ Jesus" (Philippians 2:5). The mind of Christ was a humble mind, one that was concerned for others more than Himself. It did not become fearful, faint, or weary in well-doing. We can be "more than conquerors" if we have the mind of Christ.

Memory

Memory is an integral component of the mind. Memory is the ability to keep a mental record of facts, impressions, and occurrences, along with the recording of new knowledge and experiences. If it were not for memory, we would go through the same experiences time after time and never learn anything from them. Everything would be in the present, and nothing in the past. But with memory, we use our discoveries in the past and present to steer our course in the future.

Memory is a marvelous gift from God. Some memory is short-term (such as remembering a telephone number long enough to dial it), and some is long-term (such as memorizing one's own telephone number). Long-term memory can come only by first fixing impressions in the short-term memory. This is why one needs to repeat Bible verses over and over before they will become part of the long-term memory. Even with long-term memory, there needs to be a recalling or relearning from time to time, as with periodic review of Bible passages to keep them fresh in the memory.

The Mind

After an act, an emotion, or a scene is strongly impressed on the memory, it stays there permanently. Aging people often remember impressions from long ago more easily than those of the recent past. Something that is seemingly forgotten still remains in the subconscious mind; forgetting is simply the inability to bring a memory into the conscious mind. The forgotten item is sometimes recalled in a dream or through the power of the Holy Spirit. Or a person may feel uncomfortable when in certain places or around certain people. His conscious mind has forgotten what happened; but when certain circumstances are present, the subconscious memory causes mental discomfort.

Memory and conscience are closely linked together, and they will certainly be present when God's record books are opened on the Judgment Day. The books will correspond exactly with the record of every man's conscience and memory. Nothing will be forgotten, but all will come to the light, even the deepest secrets of men's hearts. Then memory and conscience will speak either peace and rest or horror and damnation, for every man will recognize that God's records are perfectly true.

Memory and conscience are already touched by the Holy Spirit in the present life. This is an act of God's mercy, for we can face and clear our records today instead of being condemned by them at the end of life. When we repent and confess our sins, they are "open beforehand, going before to judgment" (1 Timothy 5:24); and we will be able to face the judgment bar of God with confidence instead of fear.

Memory will follow the sinner and will be one of the

torments of eternal hell. Abraham told the rich man, "Son, remember"—and he did recall his life on earth. Sinners will remember not only their unconfessed sins but also the fact that they could be in heaven if they had only repented and availed themselves of Christ's sacrifice. Such a condition is almost too dreadful to think about.

Many things may be forgotten in our memories, but one thing is certain: sin will never be forgotten. In David's case, the memory of his youthful sins apparently troubled him in adulthood (see Psalm 25:7). Perhaps at one time he had thought lightly of those sins, considering them only the errors of inexperience or ignorance or inconsideration. Now he prayed that God would not remember the sins of his youth. He wanted God not only to forgive his sins but also to forget them. Even though he had made full confession and found peace in his heart, the memory of those sins lingered in his mind.

The memory of our own sins of the past should cause us to humble ourselves and be more watchful now and in the future. We need enough grief to lead us to a sincere and full confession and then to the freedom of being forgiven. When we cease to justify ourselves and instead justify God in His right to condemn us, then alone will God justify us. He will forget our sins and remove them as far as the east is from the west. May His marvelous forgiveness kindle in us a burning love for Him and zeal in His service.

Forgiveness means that we are cleansed from sin and that the debt standing against us is blotted out. This gives rest to our consciences: even though we remember the sin, our feeling of guilt is gone because our Redeemer has cleared the record. This is in contrast to the easy penitence that is little more than regret. Easy penitence has little effect on one's life. True repentance includes serious thinking, a deep searching of the heart, and a turning away from opportunities to sin.

The Bible strongly emphasizes the duty and benefit of remembrance. In the Book of Deuteronomy alone, the Israelites were told twelve times to remember things in the past, especially God's dealings with them. To forget the past is to make ourselves ignorant of God's marvelous acts in history. It shows great ingratitude toward God, for what our fathers achieved through the power of God is a rich heritage. May we never forget those roots that have borne fruit in our lives, and may our faithfulness be worthy of remembrance in future generations.

Negative or Positive Mind

In seeking to develop Christian character, we need to have positive thoughts and attitudes if we hope to be fruitful for God. A negative approach is a deteriorating process that will take us nowhere except backward. If we have a negative mind toward people and situations, we will become negative persons. The payoff for a critical, negative person is criticism of himself. Those who are eager to point fingers at others will soon see many fingers pointing at them.

Calling attention to other people's shortcomings is often just a feeble attempt to hide our own. In the parable of the talents (see Matthew 25:14–30), the man who hid his talent said he was afraid because his master was a hard man. He who was conscious of his own fault began to find fault with his master. A person with sin in his own life will be quick to condemn sin in others, as David did when he heard about the rich man who took the poor man's only lamb. But in condemning the rich man, David condemned himself.

The whole personality degenerates when negative attitudes are present. Thus negativism not only keeps us from achieving; it also keeps us from being. We are not made for the negative but for positive achievement. Some people become so negative that they even use negative terms to assert something positive, as in "I surely can't understand how it turned out that well." Such negativism is a cancer that can ruin the success of any positive endeavor.

How did Jesus react to negative things? When He was criticized by the Pharisees for eating with publicans and sinners (see Luke 15), He did not give a negative response. Rather, He told the parables of the lost sheep, the lost coin, and the lost son, which all ended on a positive note. At the cross He turned a negative into a positive by purchasing salvation for mankind. The cross revealed man at his worst, but it portrayed God at His redemptive best.

In Luke 5 we read of three disciples who toiled all night and caught no fish. Their negative experience turned positive when Jesus filled their boats so full of fish that they began to sink. This set a pattern for their new faith and for building the church in the future. When they launched their "boats" on the sea of the new Christian era, they were almost swamped with three thousand converts on the first day of the Spirit's presence. The apostles were positive men with a positive faith, following a positive Christ and achieving positive results for a positive future.

The Mind

A person may be so afraid of making mistakes that he does not make anything worthwhile. He is confined by the fear of failure and thus a prisoner of his own fear. He may refer to his negativism as prudence, but that is only an attempt to dress it up. Prudence reckons with real dangers; negativism shies away from unlikely or imaginary dangers.

A person may have ability, intelligence, and sincere devotion but never be chosen for a position of responsibility. Is it because he has a spirit of negativism? If so, it overshadows his good qualities and leaves other people uncertain about him. The person feels unaccepted and wonders what the problem is. His negativism may even be a blind spot. We need God and our fellow men to help us see ourselves in cases like this.

If you are troubled with negativism, go over your life carefully and prayerfully, trying to deal honestly with your negative impressions and attitudes. This will probably be difficult, for negative attitudes are usually surrounded by strong defenses. Seek by the grace of God to identify each negative attitude, to break down its long-standing defenses, and to replace it with a positive and realistic attitude. You will experience rich rewards in the present and the future.

When you, by God's grace, change your outlook from negative to positive, a considerable number of negative leftovers may remain entrenched in your thinking and vocabulary. You will need to replace these with positive, constructive words. Instead of saying "I can't," say "I can"; instead of saying "I have no time," say "I'll find time." If you have looked for the ugly, begin looking for the beautiful; if you have expected people to let you down, begin trusting people and expecting the best of them. You tend to find the things you look for. If you think your abilities are too small to accomplish much, see Christ as the one who can strengthen you for anything, and He will.

At first you will miss the negative companions of the years. They have provided you with a refuge—a pitiful one, to be sure—but still a refuge from the responsibility of facing issues. Bury your dead words and attitudes, and put a "No Resurrection" sign over them. In their place, put words that are living and joyful and creative, and in the end you will appreciate them much more than your former companions.

Build your life according to the patterns you see at your highest spiritual moments, not when you are down in the valley of depression. Some make decisions when they are defeated and discouraged, and the result is a sorry product. If despondent and negative feelings come, sit still and wait until you are on the mountain with God, where you can have a clear view of the broad picture. Act on the basis of that vista, for the times when you are closest to God are your most dependable moments; the others are untrustworthy.

Some think they must respond to every urge immediately upon its appearance. Their motto is "I act on what I see, and I act now"; and this dominates their whole personality. The conflicting desires and appetites of such a person will pull him in a dozen different directions. Large amounts of his energies are wasted, and the result is a repressed, negative mentality. It is much better to wait out negative urges and to act on them only if a positive approach is unfruitful.

Negative experiences do not need to turn us into warped, negative people. If we respond to them as "more than conquerors," negative experiences can actually help to build positive, productive, and satisfying personalities.

Inferiority or Superiority Complex

Every one of us is born with a desire to be perfect, and any lack of perfection can become a source of unhappiness. We may recognize our lack of perfection by physical deformities, skin blemishes, speech defects, or other abnormalities; or it may be evident in the lack of ability to accomplish a certain thing. As we realize that we have little chance of becoming perfect, we feel inferior and may become decidedly anxious. This is the basis for the inferiority complex. Every person has known it, and no two people have experienced exactly the same one. Inferiority complexes differ widely in reasons, intensity, expressions, and methods of compensation.

People compensate for feelings of inferiority in at least three ways. One group reacts with aggression. Characteristic expressions of these people include conceit, vanity, jealousy, envy, avarice, and an overbearing, domineering spirit.

The second group takes an approach of submission. These people are so impressed with their inferiority that they surrender to the situation. Reactions of the submissive group include oversensitivity, anxiety, insecurity, and strong, irrational fears of certain things or situations, which lead to obsessions, compulsions, seclusiveness, and pessimism.

The third group compensates for feelings of inferiority

by repression. This is the practice of pushing unpleasant feelings out of the conscious mind. If the inferior feelings are associated with shame and guilt, the result is more inferior feelings and more repression. Common reactions of this group include bluff, conceit, sarcasm, bullying, intimidation, and ridicule. These reactions, along with the overbearing expressions of the first group, often appear to manifest a spirit of superiority. But a superiority complex is only a mask to cover an inferiority complex.

One of the most insidious ways of compensating for inferior feelings is the habit of gossip. There are two ways in which a person may try to gain a higher opinion of himself. One is by increasing his own status, and the other is by decreasing his neighbor's status. If a man calls attention to the faults of his neighbor, he may lower the neighbor beneath himself. This is the aim of gossip. When we gossip, we rarely have a malicious desire to injure our neighbor; we are interested mainly in helping ourselves. And we seldom gossip about a person lower on the social scale than ourselves. Gossip is usually aimed at our peers or those whose status is above ours.

Another interesting feature of gossip is that it often focuses on characteristics of which the gossiper himself is guilty. The apostle Paul spoke directly to this point. "Therefore thou are inexcusable, O man, whosoever thou art that judgest: for wherein thou judgest another, thou condemnest thyself; for thou that judgest doest the same things" (Romans 2:1).

This compensation of an inferiority complex is called projection. When one has a fault, he does not like to admit it and therefore represses it in his own mind. But

The Mind

to compensate, he projects the fault onto his neighbor, perhaps finding a little comfort in "proving" that his neighbor is no better than himself. For example, a dishonest man will invariably be suspicious of his honest neighbor. A liar refuses to believe his friend's story. An unfaithful husband tends to suspect the fidelity of his wife. It is fairly safe to say that a man can be judged as he adversely judges his neighbor.

Gossip is one of the most pitiful kinds of compensation of an inferiority complex. The gossiper only hopes to bring others down to his level, which is pathetic because it offers no real prospect of improving himself. The bringing down of another's character is only a mental scheme in the mind of the gossiper. It does nothing for the one who is the object of his gossip, unless he responds by actually improving himself. Such a response only proves that he is more strong, stable, and mature than the gossiper.

One of the most common things in the world is correction given by people who have no concrete basis for what they say. We must first have an objective view of our own faults before we are in a position to help others. Jesus plainly said in the Sermon on the Mount, "First cast out the beam out of thine own eye; and then shalt thou see clearly to cast out the mote out of thy brother's eye" (Matthew 7:5). Jesus did not deny the need of casting out the mote, but He did insist that clear vision is essential to doing it well.

Removing a beam from one's eye is no small task for even a mature character, let alone for someone with strong feelings of inferiority. But the inferior one feels he has no time for such a major operation (if he is even aware of the beam). He thinks the mote must come out of his brother's eye *now*. Obviously, no one is ready to subject himself to such an unqualified surgeon. So when the counsel of the inferior one is disregarded, it only intensifies his inferiority complex. A sincere concern for our brother is a high virtue, but it will be short-circuited if we have strong feelings of inferiority.

As incredible as it may seem, the root of the inferiority complex is pride. How can that be, when the person feels himself not superior but inferior? The essence of pride is not just an excessive *esteem* for oneself; it is an excessive *focus* on oneself. A person with an inferiority complex thinks, "*I* should make a better impression; *I* should accomplish more; *I* should measure up to higher standards." But why is it so important that *I* be an outstanding person in this world? Is it not pride, to be preoccupied with such thoughts?

The solution to an inferiority complex is Jesus Christ. Confess your pride, claim His forgiveness, and believe that you are washed pure and clean by His blood. Let guilt and shame and fear fade away as you stand justified before God by faith in Jesus Christ. He will always be with you, for He has promised, "I will never leave thee, nor forsake thee." Can we excel, can we achieve, can we be complete in Him? The answer is yes—a thousand times yes.

Jesus Christ had no inferiority complex; He focused on other people and their needs. Study His character; make it the pattern for your life. Becoming like Jesus is not too high a goal; it is within reach of anyone. However, there are no shortcuts. God will do great things to improve your character, but you must be willing to pay the price.

The Mind

Only Satan can use an inferiority complex. It is of no use to God, but He can transform it into a sweet and pleasant disposition if you let Him perform the operation. He will give you a life that brings you satisfaction and that influences others to want to follow. You owe nothing to your inferiority complex; in fact, it has already robbed you of many precious things. Overcome it by God's grace, and enter into a complete and abundant life in Christ Jesus.

Criticism and Critical Attitudes

Attitudes are mental habits to which our feelings are attached. They make or break our disposition and personality. An attitude is like a key: a wrong attitude closes a door, and a right attitude opens it. Some attitudes need to be eliminated, others improved, still others added. Changing or acquiring attitudes is a slow and difficult task that requires more patience and skill than acquiring knowledge.

We need to beware especially of critical attitudes. A good many Christians seem to think that their task is to sit on a judgment seat and give the Christian criticism of life. However, the center of the Christian faith is not a judgment seat but a cross, where men are not criticized but forgiven. People are never converted by criticism, only by the cross of Jesus Christ. Jesus did not come to criticize us but to silently bear our sins; and lo, we were melted and redeemed.

But many religious people sit as self-appointed judges day after day. Their brows are knitted and their souls perturbed; they are weighed down with the responsibility of converting the world by criticism. Their religion is a burden instead of a blessing; they are tense and uneasy instead of joyous. They are slowly but surely turning into perfect Pharisees but very poor Christians. They criticize their Christianity right out of themselves.

When we are on the prosecutor's stand, we are not in the witness box. When we are denouncing others, we are not announcing Jesus Christ. Our business is not to judge the world but to bear the Good News of Jesus Christ to all the world. "For with what judgment ye judge, ye shall be judged: and with what measure ye mete, it shall be measured to you again" (Matthew 7:2). This means that the person who dispenses judgment is laying up judgment for himself. Let us rather dispense love and love only; and if it is not received, then give out still more love. Even if there is no positive response, we will be better for having loved.

Christian people are in the business of trying to be good and do good. They are therefore tempted to point out the faults of others so that, by implication, they themselves may appear better. Strange as it may seem, the faults we see in others are often closely linked to the problems in our own lives. We recognize best what is at home with us. So if we can hardly tolerate ourselves and our own weaknesses, it is easy to see why we become critical of others.

A critical attitude toward life and people is dissolved when we get into living fellowship with Christ. Where there is communion with Christ, there are no critical attitudes toward men. Love does not make us blind to faults, but love sees the solution to faults and longs to give help. Love makes us understanding, which is more important than being understood.

We need men of compassion and construction rather than criticism. No movement, group, or church can live on criticizing others. It will die of its own negativism. The spirit of criticism in a religious movement is so alien to Christianity that it eats like acid into the souls of those who hold it and soon destroys the movement itself. For criticizers are criticized, and biters are bitten. May we find good in everything and everybody; and where we cannot find it, may we by God's grace seek to produce it by true love and faith.

Many women have made a precarious living by washing other people's clothes. And some church members make a precarious spiritual living by washing other members' clothes. "Who art thou that judgest another man's servant? to his own master he standeth or falleth. Yea, he shall be holden up: for God is able to make him stand" (Romans 14:4). This penetrating statement says that a critical person may be condemning someone whom the Master commends, and thus his actions may be at cross-purposes with the work of Christ Himself. God forbid that such should be true of us.

How should we respond when criticism comes? The first thing is to ask ourselves, Is it true? If so, acknowledge to yourself and your friend that it is a fair criticism and that you will try to profit from it. Actually, those who give healthy criticism are some of the greatest helpers to our spiritual lives. If we do not have these unhired friends, we become the poorer for it. Our critics may be the very hammers that God is using to beat us into shape, even if they are people whom we consider less mature than ourselves.

Look for wisdom in criticism; it may not be mere fault-finding but friendly advice. Our critics may see in us some defect or inconsistency that we are blind to and that definitely needs to be improved. Train your mind to sift out critical remarks that are simple nonsense from those that contain true wisdom. Responding positively to wisdom in a criticism can make us better people and enhance God's cause.

If only one person raises an issue, there may or may not be merit in what he says. But if two or more people say the same thing, we had better pay attention. Rather then trying to justify ourselves, we can say, "Oh, I can see why that might bother you," or "Thanks for bringing that to my attention. I will address it right away." This takes our critic off the defensive, and we are better able to see the truth about ourselves.

Some criticism may be harsh and unfair, often because of a faulty understanding of your intentions or actions. In this case, breathe a prayer for your critic and for yourself. It is much harder to hate a man after you have prayed for him. If you want to cure him of his ignorance and ill will, you will need to keep all your thoughts and words toward him bathed in prayer. A prayerless thought can quickly become a resentful thought. Then maintain an inner spiritual dignity that will keep you from descending to his level through retaliation.

Further, look for ways to do him good. Your critic will have his shield up, awaiting your return blow. Strike him where he is unguarded: return good for evil. The poison of the slanderer's words will return to him; that will be more than enough payback for his malice. In loving our enemies, in turning the other cheek as our Lord commanded and demonstrated, we rise above our enemies and become superior to them; we may even win them in the end. And if not, we have preserved our own souls.

Sometimes we owe it to ourselves and the critics to clarify things by an explanation. This can be done by a letter, but it is best to write it in prayer and then lay it aside for a day or two. Remember that Satan cannot cast out Satan; and if we act like the devil, we can never help to free people from the devil's power. Be sure to write the kind of letter that you would like to receive.

But perhaps you should not answer at all, and let Christ answer for you. When the scribes and Pharisees murmured against the disciples, Jesus answered them much more effectively than the disciples could have done (see Luke 5:30–32). Many a person has apologized for harsh criticism after the Holy Spirit rebuked him; whereas if the recipient had become defensive or responded in kind, the critic would have launched an even stronger attack. Remember that Christ knows the best way to deal with men's hearts.

People can spot inconsistency a mile away. If we put on an air of prim perfection, we set ourselves up as a target for criticism. But if we make it clear that we are just as human as others, people around us will be more tolerant of our blunders.

When you are about to criticize another, ask three questions: Is it true? Is it necessary? Is it kind? If all three answers are yes, then prayerfully and carefully approach your brother and seek to help him. Be especially careful not to become petty, always seeking out something to correct in your brother. We should be more inclined to compliment and encourage than to correct. We need not fear that we will cause people to be proud, for compliments usually make sincere souls feel humbled rather than exalted.

Jesus Christ is the center of the Christian life; and as believers, we should revolve around that center. If other people and their faults become the center of our operations, we not only wear out ourselves but we also expend time and effort that could be put to much better use. Worst of all, we no longer serve the One who gave His life for the forgiveness of our own sins. We can afford only an occasional glance at the faults of others: our primary gaze must focus on the grace and goodness of Jesus. May all our criticisms of people turn into prayers rising heavenward for them.

Giving and Receiving Counsel

"Where no counsel is, the people fall: but in the multitude of counsellors there is safety" (Proverbs 11:14). This proverb is based on the assumption that somewhere in a group of counselors, a safe and wise answer may be found. It does not assure that any group of humans as a whole can always give wise counsel. If it did, perfect truth and wisdom could be found by simply taking the voice of the majority in any body of counselors. Rather, the proverb suggests allowing each counselor to freely express his opinion based on the facts available. The most difficult thing then is for the group to recognize and follow the counsel that is truly safe and wise.

It follows that free and open discussion is essential to

The Mind

understanding a given situation and to gaining a broad view of it. A number of safeguards need to be in place so that the discussion will produce the best results. All prejudice and unsanctified motives must be avoided, along with any abuse of power. Truth and right must never be suppressed in favor of those who hold eminent positions. Free and open discussion must be a means to an end and not an end in itself, or it may be exploited by those who insist on promoting their own opinions.

The desire to please or to be pleased is the enemy of sound counsel. A good counselor cannot value his head or reputation above his honesty; he must speak the truth regardless of the outcome. Even if a man knows that his counsel is right but will be displeasing, he must not change it to avert the disgrace or suffering that will follow. The prophet Micaiah provided an excellent example of this when he was brought before King Ahab (see 1 Kings 22).

Any counsel must be entirely in the interest of the one who receives it. To give counsel with selfish motives for the counselor's advantage is both dishonest and repulsive. Good counsel is sincere and honest in itself. It is appropriate and timely, and it works to the benefit of all involved.

A counselor must be sure he knows all the pertinent facts before he gives his counsel. For example, to assume that one is guilty of misconduct or is disqualified for a certain privilege, without considering the circumstances involved, is nothing less than cruel. Injustice in counsel deprives it of the good judgment needed to make it effective. If the counselor says anything that makes the other person feel inferior for his lack of knowledge or experience, it will only spoil his opportunity to render effective counsel in the future.

A good counselor to a distressed, longing, hungry soul will be a Christian who has himself struggled with sin, who understands the human nature and its depravity, but who also knows the renewing grace of God and the redeeming love of Jesus Christ. He must be endued with wisdom from above, which is "first pure, then peaceable, gentle, and easy to be intreated, full of mercy and good fruits, without partiality, and without hypocrisy" (James 3:17).

How can we be sure of receiving good counsel when we need it? Above all, we must be known to love and desire the truth. If a man lives in pretense, shuns the truth, and hates to be disturbed in his pursuit of pleasure, any counsel that he receives will probably be after his liking. But a man who loves the truth will both speak truth and hear words of truth and wise counsel.

There is safety in seeking counsel from several individuals. Different people can evaluate a situation from different angles because of their varied levels of experience, maturity, and ability. We can feel safe especially when a united Scriptural brotherhood makes a decision or helps us to make a personal decision. Such counsel carries a measure of wisdom that cannot be disregarded without paying the consequences.

Some who seek advice are unable to distinguish between competing counsels. The power to discern good counsel varies greatly in men. Some possess it as a natural gift, some acquire it only after long experience, and some never do get hold of it. One of the best ways to gain the power of discernment is to become familiar with the Word of the living God, whose counsels are holy, wise, and safe. No counsel will take us in the wrong direction if it is in line with the principles of the Word.

Giving and receiving counsel is normal in every period of life. The young are at a stage when they need counsel the most but may want it the least. They face momentous decisions, such as buying a vehicle, choosing an occupation, and choosing a marriage partner. They need plenty of wholesome counsel from godly parents, ministers, and other faithful believers. Young people have many noble aspirations, but they need to be tempered by the wisdom of those who have more experience. Too many people, young and old, prefer using a trial-and-error method rather than seeking counsel. This may work sometimes, but often it results in paying dearly for lessons that could have been learned from the experience of others.

Both givers and receivers of counsel will profit the most if they are truly humble. A humble person has a healthy awareness of his own limitations. He realizes that he is not wise enough to make his own decisions or to help others with their decisions, without the help of God and his fellow men. Humbly giving and receiving counsel is part of honestly recognizing our needs and preferring others before ourselves.

The counsel we receive today will enable us to give good counsel tomorrow. As we apply sound counsel to the situations we face, we become wiser and better able to help others in similar situations. How sad it is that many people lightly throw aside the counsel offered for their eternal welfare! But those who are "more than conquerors" will hear the words of good counsel, apply them diligently, and dwell forever among the wise.

Silence in Speech

Words are not trivialities; they are the normal fruit of the heart. We speak in words, and we think in words. Impressions made in the mind will naturally find expression in words. If a person has no way to communicate his thoughts to others, he becomes greatly frustrated and may even develop emotional and mental problems.

Words reveal not only thoughts but also character. What the heart is full of will come out of the mouth (see Luke 6:45). Therefore, wrong speech must be cured in the heart and not in the tongue. Cutting down the tree will never change the root. Nothing but the grace of God will heal the bitter spring of a bad heart. Let the heart be converted, and the fruit of the tongue will be pure and wholesome.

"The prudent shall keep silence" (Amos 5:13). A wise man is not always silent, but he knows when to be. If there is nothing to say, it is the eloquence of discretion to remain silent. Indeed, silence is sometimes the best way to express feelings too deep for words. Men of few words are often the best men. Talking comes by nature, silence by understanding.

Silence is always better than haphazard speech. Often we say more by saying less, and say less by saying more. In some cases (such as a dispute), a thing may have gone so far that it does no good to keep on talking; it may even do harm. We need the wisdom of God to discern when it is so.

"In the multitude of words there wanteth not sin: but he that refraineth his lips is wise" (Proverbs 10:19). The eagerness to talk is a mark of a shallow mind. He who is ever speaking is sure to say idle and vain words before very long. It is much better to weigh our words carefully and then speak them at the right moment. "A word spoken in due season, how good is it!" (Proverbs 15:23).

Words of wisdom and love have the beauty of the graces that inspire them. A man who speaks such words is one who thinks, who ponders what he knows, who considers the feelings of others, and who takes the trouble to look backward and forward. He considers not only the matter but also the manner of his speech.

A successful man is one who works his tongue little, his hands much, and his brain most. Remember that we have two ears but only one tongue, that we may hear twice as much as we speak. Also consider that our ears are always open but our mouth can be shut. Our ears will be of little benefit if we are talking all the time.

We often speak merely to gratify the curiosity of those present or to use the advantage of knowledge we happen to possess. The words rise to our lips and condemn us before they are fully spoken. This kind of careless speech may do untold harm. Let us remember that our brother's reputation and welfare is in our charge, and one whisper can destroy it all. It is not always our duty to say what we know; it is often our duty to be silent.

Finally, we need to be silent before God. "Be still, and know that I am God." Our finest worship before God may be silent reverence and submission in the presence of His authority. "The LORD is in his holy temple: let all the earth keep silence before him" (Habakkuk 2:20).

The Renewing of the Mind

The New Testament gives the following lists of sins that believers are to avoid.

Seven in which we must not engage (Romans 13:13, 14)

Six with which we must not associate (1 Corinthians 5:9–11)

Eleven that must not be present in the church (2 Corinthians 12:20, 21)

Seventeen that will keep us from inheriting the kingdom of God (Galatians 5:19–21)

Nine in which sinners live but saints must not (Ephesians 4:25–31)

Six that should not be named among the saints (Ephesians 5:3, 4)

Twelve that we must mortify or put off (Colossians 3:5–9)

Nineteen from which we must turn away (2 Timothy 3:1–5)

Nine from which we are saved (Titus 3:3–5)

Five that we must lay aside (1 Peter 2:1)

These lists name a total of 101 sins that are potential pitfalls for Christians. There is some repetition in the lists, but the question remains: How can a person ever have victory over all these sins? It could seem like a vain hope.

The secret of Christian victory is to put on Jesus Christ and the mind of Christ. "But put ye on the Lord Jesus Christ, and make not provision for the flesh, to fulfil the lusts thereof" (Romans 13:14). Jesus was tempted with all these sins as we are, yet He was able to live a perfect, sinless life. The same Spirit that was present with Him is with us today, and He can keep us from sin every day and every hour.

As Christians, we received the mind of Christ when we

The Mind

received Christ Himself. We have a new, divine nature that cannot and will not sin. But we also have the old, carnal nature that loves to sin better than anything else. We must learn to say no to the old nature and yes to the new nature.

The old nature can make very strong demands, sometimes so strong that a person wonders if he is even saved. "I wouldn't have such a desire to sin if I were really a Christian." This lie is one of Satan's favorite tactics for getting us to fall. A strong desire to sin does not prove that the new nature is absent; it simply means that the old nature is crying louder at the moment. The thing to do is not to yield but to deny its demands by exercising the mind of Christ through the power of the Holy Spirit. The Bible speaks of this as crucifying the flesh.

True repentance is the starting point for a renewed mind. Repentance is not reform or repression, but a complete turning away from our sins, a changing of our attitude toward them, and a turning to God for mercy. This leads to being "transformed by the renewing of your mind," which is the only way to find "that good, and acceptable, and perfect, will of God" (Romans 12:2). The renewed mind is a mind of peace, joy, and rest.

When there is a strong, constant battle to subdue, suppress, and fight back wrong desires, it is evidence that there has not been true repentance and renewing of the mind. The person may be secretly fond of a forbidden delight that he is unwilling to give up. He may try to push the thing out of his conscious mind, but the desire stays in his subconscious mind and continues to trouble him. The wrong desire may be repressed so long that the person is not aware of it, but the Holy Spirit will be faithful to bring it to his attention if he is honest. For the Scriptures say, "If in any thing ye be otherwise minded [than wholeheartedly pressing toward the mark], God shall reveal even this unto you" (Philippians 3:15).

Many a person has awakened in the morning tired and depressed because he struggled in the subconscious mind all night. He was working while he slept. The solution is not continued repression but sincere repentance, recognizing the forbidden thing for the evil that it is and renouncing it with the whole heart. If one has not quite the will to do that, God can even help him to become willing. "For it is God which worketh in you both to will and to do of his good pleasure" (Philippians 2:13).

The renewed mind is needed especially to overcome sins of the disposition. These include envy, pride, worry, selfishness, impatience, irritability, discontent, a fault-finding spirit, and an uncontrolled temper. Few things will hinder our Christian testimony as effectively as a sour disposition and a sharp tongue. In fact, we sometimes meet sinners who are more kind, gracious, and considerate than some professing Christians.

It is time to stop excusing these "minor" sins, to admit frankly that we have failed, and to claim the power of God for victory. With the mind of Christ, we can be "more than conquerors" over dispositional sins and all other sins.

CHAPTER 7

The Emotions

Nature of Emotions

As stated before, the soul consists of the will, the mind, and the emotions. The will is intended to be in control; but for some people, life seems to revolve around the impulses of emotion. However, emotions are the most unstable and least dependable part of man's soul. The reason is that emotions rise and fall with changing circumstances.

Emotions have a strong effect because they cause pain or pleasure. This often convinces people that something is a fact simply because it *feels* that way. "If I feel well, I must be well. If I feel like a fool, I must be a fool." Obviously, such feelings may be far removed from the real facts.

Emotions often swing like a pendulum from one extreme to the other. This is especially true of great joy or exhilaration, which is commonly followed by feelings of despondency or even deep depression. Our emotions must come under the sanctifying power of the Holy Spirit and be subservient to our wills, which are ultimately subject to God's will. We cannot experience the power of the Holy Spirit if we live by the impulse of emotions.

As children of God, we must learn to distinguish between our emotions and the Spirit's voice. The roaring of emotions may be so loud that we cannot hear the Spirit speaking. But when the Spirit ceases to have control, emotions will take control, and soon we will be walking after the flesh instead of the Spirit. We may even think we are guided by inspirations from the Holy Spirit when we are merely following our emotional impulses.

How can we tell the difference? Emotions are triggered by outward influences, whereas inspirations originate from the Holy Spirit working within. For example, we experience great awe when we see a marvel of creation, and strong feelings of happiness when we meet a loved one from a distant place. These are emotions caused by outward events. But inspiration from the Holy Spirit comes from within, apart from external causes. It does not require the stimulus of a scenic wonder or the presence of a loved one.

When a believer first finds new life in Christ, he often becomes attached to the Lord with a great and strong affection. He may feel so close to Jesus that it seems he can almost touch Him with his hands. A fire burns in his soul, bringing unspeakable joy and making him think he is almost in heaven. Bible reading is bliss, and prayer is pleasure. He wishes he could shut the door of his closet and commune with the Lord forever. His delight is so intense that neither tongue nor pen can fully express it.

Can this kind of exuberant joy go on forever? Many a new believer has been dismayed and grieved when it faded after a time. What happened? He reads his Bible, but the cherished sweetness is gone. He continues to pray, but he finds himself empty after a few sentences. Some people react by blaming God for the sudden end of their blissful experience. Others think they must have sinned, and they painstakingly scrutinize their lives. If only they knew what was wrong, they could confess their sin and have the joy return. But all is in vain.

Soon the believer is plagued with doubt and discouragement, and he loses interest in spiritual things. Whereas he could formerly read his Bible and pray for hours, it all seems forced and uninviting now. What is the use of praying when God does not hear his cries? His zeal for holy living wanes, and he cannot claim the joyous victory he wants to know. He becomes careless and negligent about spiritual things. He knows it should not be this way, but he cannot help himself.

As the struggle goes on, something may happen that brings the believer back to his former experience. Perhaps he gains a sudden, new insight while reading the Bible or during a soul-searching prayer. The coveted feeling returns; the presence of God feels near again; the fire in his bosom is glowing once more. What a wonderful feeling! He determines that the despondent feelings will not come back again; he will give all diligence to keep up his faith and fellowship with God. Never again will he sink so low and almost lose his anchor in Christ.

Such a believer thinks he is on a spiritual peak when he feels close to God but in a deep valley when the wonderful feeling is absent. His spiritual walk is irregular, up one day and down another. Is such a life to be accepted as the norm for Christians? Certainly not. Then what can we learn from this all-too-common experience?

"More Than Conquerors"

God grants us great joy when we first believe, as a way of drawing us very close to Himself. He fills us with a marvelous sense of love and peace so that we love Him and delight in Him. Then He stands back, so to speak, to see whether we will keep on serving Him even when our feelings change. God wants us to understand ourselves and to see how inadequate we are without Him. He wants our faith to rest on Him alone, not on our emotions or any other thing.

Facts and truth must be the basis of our assurance, not feelings and sensations. Actually, living by either the up or the down feelings is living by the emotions. Neither is a reliable gauge of our relationship with God. For a believer may be growing in his Christian life even when he feels that he is making no progress at all. Trials and difficulties in the Christian life seldom generate high sensations, yet they contribute to Christian maturity as nothing else can. We gain some of our deepest convictions and greatest spiritual triumphs in times of adversity—when our feelings may be at their lowest.

We live by true faith as our wills choose to follow the Holy Spirit's guidance through our spirits. We can do His bidding without the slightest support from our fleeting emotions. But if we allow emotions to stifle the spirit and the will, we can have no spiritual power to do as we ought. We then rely on emotions to propel us, and soon our Christian lives are void of strength and vitality.

We must ask ourselves, Do our feelings of joy and exultation come from a solid relationship with God, or have they become a god to us? Do we love God, or do we love that delightful feeling of joy? We will face this test when everything is removed that excited our emotions. If we do truly love God, we will not become bitter but will say as Job did in his anguish, "Though he slay me, yet will I trust in him" (Job 13:15).

Strong, unwholesome emotions will bring internal tensions that cause mental and physical havoc. This is like racing the engine while sitting in a parked car, burning up fuel and putting needless wear on the engine. Surgeons have performed many operations when the trouble was not structural at all but was caused by emotions. Our emotions need to be straight if we want to be whole in body, mind, and spirit.

How can emotions be transformed? Ecclesiastes 1:15 says that something crooked cannot be made straight, but that is not true of our emotions. The only way to straighten twisted emotions is to surrender them by faith into the hands of God and then relax. Let go of your tense, struggling attitudes, receive the grace of God, and cultivate constructive emotions by thinking on things of love, beauty, and truth. Wholesome thoughts will be followed by wholesome emotions.

One who walks in the Spirit is governed by principles of truth and fixed moral standards. Right is right and wrong is wrong, regardless of the circumstances and feelings involved. Those who would conquer must live not by changing emotions but by solid principles and facts.

Guilt

If there is anything that man would like to be free from, it is the guilt that hangs over his soul and clouds his emotions. Every man carries within his bosom the realization of God's judgment on his sins. The resulting guilt may seem like a hindrance to his moral happiness; but no, it is rather a blessing. Guilt is to the soul as pain is to the body. God has designed that guilt enter man's experience after sin so that he longs for reconciliation.

The conscious guilt in man's heart is expressed in words such as "I should not have done that" and "I have failed to do what I should." Under every sky, in every age, men face these sad and solemn facts. They may possess exclusive knowledge of the transgression, but that is no consolation. In fact, if a person knows that he is solely responsible for a certain wrong, it only adds to his guilt if someone else is blamed for it. Public opinion never avails to change the fact or to relieve the burden of conscious guilt.

The conscious sense of guilt is not always present in man; but when it is brought home to him, it has a depressing influence and seriously affects the transactions of life. A guilty conscience not only makes cowards of us, but it also robs life of brightness, sullies the springs of hope, and fetters the faculties. No man can make the most of his life as long as unrepented and unforgiven sin haunts his spirit.

The guilty flee when no one pursues (see Proverbs 28:1). Guilt is of such a nature that it trembles at a sound, it condemns when no one finds fault, and it defends when no one accuses. The guilty has an accuser in his own conscience, which follows him everywhere and from which he cannot escape any more than he can flee from himself. The awful voice is always there, clamoring against his guilt and shaking the very foundations of his soul. Sometimes it utterly unnerves a man even though outwardly he dwells in perfect security.

The knowledge of truth does not relieve guilt; in fact, it increases the guilt of those who will not follow truth. Balaam knew the true God and the way of right. But in going against that knowledge, he aggravated his guilt and sealed his doom. It is worse than useless to know Christian truth unless we are willing to obey it, because then we only deceive ourselves (see James 1:22). For one oppressed with guilt, the only wise thing is to humble himself before God and seek cleansing, forgiveness, and overcoming power through Christ.

One who finds himself guilty should voluntarily do all that is necessary to clear his wrong. Self-examination and confession may be a most humiliating process, but it is the only way to find forgiveness and restoration. The more we have from God, the clearer our vision of His truth and will. The higher our status in the sight of men, the more God requires of us, and the more heinous will be our guilt if we depart from His ways. If a priest sinned, his transgression was attended with more guilt and required a greater sacrifice than did the sins of the common people. The same principle applies to church leaders today. Their position, power, and privileges are tied to a greater accountability and greater guilt if they fall.

A word of warning must be given against the methods of secular psychologists in dealing with guilt. When they find a person in conflict with himself, having high ideals but low ethics, they often dismiss the whole of moral and spiritual values and try to unify the person on the level of conduct. This only introduces a new conflict and causes even greater disruption and disunity. Moral and spiritual obligations cannot be dismissed by a wave of the hand or a slick theory. The key to relieving guilt is not to overcome one's inhibitions but to obtain pardon from a holy God.

The moment we feel conviction for sin, we are guilty before God. This is true whether the transgression was willful or unintentional. Regret and confession, as good as they are, can never clear the offense or remove the guilt. But as we acknowledge our transgressions and receive cleansing by the blood of Christ, we become "more than conquerors" over sin, guilt, and shame.

Fear

Our civilization, in general, lies under a pall of fear and anxiety. Fear may be defined in three categories: natural fear, unnatural fear, and godly fear. Natural fear operates when the five senses bring warnings of danger. We see or hear something that indicates a hazard, and fear moves us to protect ourselves. We feel the heat from a hot stove, and we are careful to keep our distance. When we smell the odor of gas, fear warns us not to strike a match. A certain flavor in food immediately warns us that it could be harmful. Natural fear is a built-in defense for mankind's own protection.

Unnatural fear is a fear that brings dread and torment. It can be implanted in a person through a past experience, such as a tragedy in childhood. Another source is alarming stories and old superstitions. Unnatural fear may be fed by one's peers and surroundings and be nurtured in one's own thought life; and with time, it can grow into an oppressive weight of torment and anguish. No doubt many of us have experienced some degree of unnatural fear.

Godly fear is demonstrated by reverence and respect

The Emotions

for God. Sinners may have this fear to some degree; for example, one thief on the cross said to the other, "Dost not thou fear God?" (Luke 23:40). Godly fear in ungodly people is a restraining influence that puts certain limits on their actions. But the fear of God is primarily a characteristic of the born-again child of God. He fears to displease God, yet his service to God is driven by love rather than cowardly fear. "There is no fear in love; but perfect love casteth out fear: because fear hath torment" (1 John 4:18).

Fear and anxiety are like sand in the machinery of life. We are naturally made to live not by fear but by faith; only in this way can we breathe and move freely. Faith is not something imposed on us but written intrinsically in our being; we cannot live without it. To live by fear and worry is to live against nature.

Natural man has various ways of dealing with the torment of fear. One method is that of seeking escape, as suggested by many people's frenzied running from one place to another and from one thing to another. This provides no relief but only brings more insecurity and fear. Neither will narcotics, alcohol, and tranquilizers afford an escape from the anguish of fear. They may deaden and ease it for a time, but the fear always returns in full force afterward.

Some try to hide their fears behind a façade of some kind. Laughter and merriment may conceal a person's fears from others, but it will never remove them. Or the fearful one may take the opposite approach and put on a stone face. This denial of feelings is an attempt to keep from being hurt; but the pressure must and will find release somehow, and it may do so at a most unexpected time and place. If conscious fears are forced into the subconscious mind, they will gnaw like a rat at the whole of one's being.

A related method is to disguise our fears. A man with a heart full of fears may put on a great show of bravado and daring. The one who feels the most inferior on the inside may do the loudest boasting on the outside. Do not be fooled; such people are seldom as strong and bold as they appear.

Some people try to fight fear, but this method will also fail. There is an unwritten law of the mind that "whatever gets your attention gets you"; and if your fears get your attention, though it be a fighting attention, they will defeat you. Fighting fear and anxiety tends to be a battle in the dark, for we do not know what our enemy is or where he will strike next.

One of the most common fears is fear of the unknown future. We can be glad that the future is unknown. If we saw all the good things coming to us, we would sit down and degenerate; and if we saw all the bad things, we would be paralyzed. The fear of death is naturally the greatest of all fears; many live a life overshadowed by the fear of death. Thank God that Jesus has triumphed over death! He said, "I am the resurrection, and the life: he that believeth in me . . . shall never die." Why should we fear death when we have Jesus? Those who live in Christ will die in Him.

Let us consider a few steps out of fear. First, if you have fears, do not be afraid to admit the fact. Do not drive them into your subconscious mind by ignoring them. Next, give up all justification of your fears. See anxieties as foolish (they cannot change anything), and cease playing the fool. Then surrender all your fears and anxieties into the hands of God.

This is easy to say, but doing it may be far from simple. It may mean giving up a whole life strategy. You have been depending on your fears and anxieties, and to renounce them means a complete reversal in life. You will be tempted to compromise, half giving them up and half keeping them in your hands, but this only spells failure. You need to give up all responsibility for matters you cannot control, and let God work things out from now on.

Set your eyes on God and not on yourself and your fears. Looking to God produces faith; looking to yourself and your circumstances creates fear. Try doing even the things you shrank from doing for fear of failure; by God's grace you can move forward and find success. Convince yourself that most of your fears are imaginary, and look life straight in the face.

Let us fear God, and we will have nothing else to fear. "The fear of the LORD is a fountain of life, to depart from the snares of death" (Proverbs 14:27). May we not succumb to anxiety and apprehension, but be "more than conquerors" over fear through Him.

Grief

Nobody escapes grief, for it comes to us all. Even "Jesus wept" at the grave of Lazarus. People respond to grief in different ways. Some immediately explode with emotion. Others harbor the sorrow within and brood over it, and the full realization of the loss does not come until much later. To still others, the shock is so great that it brings a sense of unreality. To weep is impossible; but months later, they may break into tears at the most unexpected moments.

"More Than Conquerors"

We may have our lives wrapped up in our loved ones to such an extent that when death comes to those loved ones, we find it hard to acknowledge that they are really gone. It may be difficult to reorder our lives to go on without our loved ones, and we may feel incapable of making new friends or finding new interests. Grief comes to all; it will sour some and sweeten others. Which will it do for you?

There is no doubt that grief will produce an aching loneliness for the one who is denied the intimacy of a very close companion. But to retreat into the seclusion of one's own soul is to surrender one's claim upon life, and to feed upon loneliness is to feed on ashes. We need to cultivate relationships, for we are made to associate with others and be involved in their lives.

It takes time to build a relationship, and it takes time to let it go. When our loved ones are taken, it takes time to heal. But to be completely absorbed in one's grief will paralyze a person as few other things can. It is a dark cloak that surrounds the person until he can scarcely look out and see others. Some people allow grief to spoil months and years of living. They feel that anything else would be disloyal to the absent loved one, so they drape their bodies and souls in mourning and withdraw into a self-made prison of grief and sorrow.

How shall we deal with grief and sorrow? If we can accept the fact that these will come to every person at one time or another, we will be spared the feeling, when grief comes, that we are being singled out for persecution. Then we are less likely to react with aggrieved self-pity or to assume a martyr mentality, which only produces further unhappiness. Neither should we try to escape sorrow by any illusions or subterfuges, such as imagining that the departed one is merely away from home for a time. Denial will turn out in the end to be worse than the grief itself.

May we take our loneliness and grief into the quietness of God's presence, and there surrender them fully and permanently into His hands. Prayer will moderate grief, for it will bring us into fellowship with God; and in fellowship with Him our loneliness finds relief. But prayer just for ourselves will not overcome loneliness; we must also intercede for the needs and sorrows of others. Taking on the griefs of other people will help to ease the hurt of our own griefs.

Let us consider some steps in the recovery from grief. First, acknowledge that the death really happened. Allow yourself to experience the pain of losing. Deliberately take memory trips to places and events connected to your relationship with the person now gone. Keep a journal in which you write your feelings and thoughts about the lost relationship. Share your feelings with a trusted person who will listen nonjudgmentally. Do not hold back your tears. Weeping with another person is more therapeutic than weeping alone.

Do not pretend the grief is not real or hard. We hurt because we have loved and cared, and that loving and caring we will never regret. The greater our capacity to love, the greater our capacity to grieve. God meant that we should love and care deeply and that it should stand true and faithful to the end of life.

It will be difficult for you not to ask why this must be.

"More Than Conquerors"

God knows why, and that may be as comforting to us as if we knew a thousand reasons. May God give us hearts that are quiet and patient and uncomplaining, and help us to bear the weight of our unintelligible sorrow. This is the only world in which a Christian can suffer; may we suffer patiently and meekly. All suffering will be over by and by; may we glorify God in sorrow while we can.

Grief and loss indeed bring great pain; but if there is no admixture of bitterness or resentment or self-pity, such pain is clean and healing. The pain of grief may seem constant at first; then later it may come in waves that almost overwhelm us with their intensity. How can we endure the force of these awful surges? "The eternal God is thy refuge, and underneath are the everlasting arms" (Deuteronomy 33:27). Cling firmly to the Rock of Ages in such times; God will hear your anguished cry. "Lord, I don't understand it, but I know it is right. You make no mistakes." See Psalm 61:2.

Some find the pain too great to say good-bye to the relationship. But saying good-bye is an essential part of healing. Do not say good-bye to the person or the memories or the hope of future reunion. But say good-bye to the relationship as it was and can be no longer. This must come by degrees; you cannot expect to do it all at once.

A loss of faith during grief is very common, but it should be very temporary. It may be hard to pray and read the Bible, but continue even though it is hard. Never let spiritual truths come under question while experiencing loss and grief. We can be "more than conquerors" in the face of grief as we walk with Jesus our Lord through the "valley of the shadow of death."

The Emotions

Comfort

It is good to go to the house of mourning, but few know how to conduct themselves when there. Job's friends were such men. "Then Job answered and said, I have heard many such things: miserable comforters are ye all. Shall vain words have an end? . . . I also could speak as ye do: if your soul were in my soul's stead, I could heap up words against you, and shake mine head at you" (Job 16:1–4).

We often make the mistake of thinking we must say something to a grieving one. But the most sincere phrases may sound harsh on strained ears. Comfort and sympathy are often best communicated by silence, for this shows our friend that we have entered into his distress. It would have been better if Job's friends had gone home after seven days of silence, for their ensuing words ruined all the good that they intended. The greatest need of one in sorrow is sympathy, not advice such as "Look to the Lord." True sympathy brings an unbidden tear, or simply places a hand on the shoulder, or gives a look of heartfelt compassion.

Why is it that we often fail to provide real consolation? Though we may mean well, all too often we are affected by selfishness, the great enemy of sympathy. We think so much of ourselves—our own ideas, abilities, and comfort—that it is no marvel when our efforts to comfort others fall flat to the ground. Why should the misfortune of another give us a right to pose as his counselors? He is more fitted to be our teacher, for he has been in the school of affliction. When we try to comfort by telling a long tale of our own woes, we only add to the distress of the afflicted one. It takes only a few words to tell someone that we are deeply hurting too. The grieving one can soon detect whether we really feel with him.

When indiscreet consolation is pressed upon a heart full of sadness, it only increases the distress and renders the grief more painful. Usually the sorrowing one is so full of his own tormenting thoughts that he has no room for the comments of untimely advisers. You cannot be fair with a grieving one until you are willing to enter into his pain and suffer with him. Nothing is more distressing than sympathy sung to an uncaring tune. "As he that taketh away a garment in cold weather, and as vinegar upon nitre, so is he that singeth songs to an heavy heart" (Proverbs 25:20).

Many seek comfort by reasoning that this case is no worse than what others are going through. They may say, "It couldn't be helped" or "It could have been worse." Some try to simply forget their distress and grief, while others try to get their minds off their sorrow by pursuing work or pleasure. May we see comfort not as a mechanical process but as a gift that God gives to His children. When we are stricken, may we seek God's touch first of all, simply sinking into His everlasting arms. "And as thy days, so shall thy strength be."

As every man is subject to sorrow, so every man is eligible for God's comfort. Indeed, He is the God of all comfort (see 2 Corinthians 1:3). This comfort is more than condolence and consolation; it is more than sympathy that soothes our torn and bleeding hearts. It is One called alongside in the extremity of our sorrow and affliction. God Himself will come to our side, bolster our souls, and strengthen our faith and peace.

The Emotions

The comfort of God includes a variety of blessings. One is the comfort of God's Word, the "patience and comfort of the scriptures." A second is the "comfort of love," God's amazing love for us. A third is the comfort of God's presence, for He has said, "I will never leave thee, nor forsake thee." A fourth is the comfort of Christ's resurrection and His second coming; "wherefore comfort one another with these words." Together, these minister a soothing, divine comfort that only the children of God can know.

Believers have the comfort of fellow saints, who help to bear their burdens and share their sorrows. People without the support of church relations must often endure their sorrows and adversities all alone. Faithful brethren in Christ are our best friends in the flesh. They are the divine Spirit robed in flesh like ours, and many of them have experienced grief and adversity equal to or greater than our own.

Those who have gone through sorrow themselves can best express unutterable words in silence. Let the mother who has children in heaven comfort the mother who sits so still, with broken heart, beside her baby's casket. Send a widowed mother to cheer the newly widowed wife. The plant of healing sympathies will blossom and bear fruit out of our wounds and tears and losses. There is an unconscious influence that reaches far and deep into the bleeding hearts of those who mourn.

Jesus Christ is our supreme example of comfort and consolation. He exchanged the form of God for the form of a servant and was made in the likeness of men (see Philippians 2:6, 7). He was "a man of sorrows, and acquainted with grief," and He has "borne our griefs, and carried our sorrows." This He experienced so that someday we could be in heaven with Him, where "God shall wipe away all tears from [our] eyes; and there shall be no more death, neither sorrow, nor crying" (Revelation 21:4). On that day, all our earthly sorrows will melt into nothing in the eternal comfort of God's glorious presence.

Depression

Why do people become depressed? What causes this psychological disorder, gloom, and sadness? We tend to think that depression is mainly a problem of unbelievers, but Christians can also be affected; spiritual faith does not guarantee immunity. Depression often follows a major loss in a person's life—a job loss, a financial reverse, or the death of a loved one. This means that every person has the potential of becoming depressed.

Other things may also trigger depression. From without comes the pressure to achieve, to fulfill expectations, to strive for perfection, to overcome undesirable habits—in short, to be the ideal man or woman. Add to this the internal pressure of fear, anxiety, self-doubt, and the need for acceptance and approval. If a Christian does not have the spiritual and emotional means to deal with these stresses, he may sink into a mire of depression.

A person suffering from depression may become so physically and mentally exhausted that he experiences an emotional collapse. This breakdown may be classified as mild, moderate, or severe. In a mild breakdown, the person may become weepy, feel extremely tired and tense, lose confidence in himself, lose appetite, and have trouble sleeping. In a moderate breakdown, these same

The Emotions

symptoms are present but with greater intensity, and the person is partially disabled in meeting the everyday responsibilities of living.

In a severe breakdown, the person is unable to function at all; he is severely or totally disabled. Perhaps his hands tremble, and he feels trapped; he wonders if there is any way out, and he may entertain thoughts of suicide. This kind of behavior is called neurotic. The person maintains contact with his surroundings, but his impressions are confused and unrealistic. He perceives reality not as it is but as he is afraid it is or as he wishes it were.

Once a person is a captive of this black mood, he becomes progressively isolated, more dependent on others, unable to think for himself, and unable to make decisions. This condition does not just come and then leave; it is something beyond the person's control. For that reason, the person needs help from someone who is experienced in the field of emotional and spiritual recovery.

The sufferer often receives much advice from well-meaning people. He may hear things like "Why don't you snap out of it?" or "What you need is more faith!" or "Pull yourself together!" or "Look on the bright side!" Such expressions are more destructive than helpful, for a person in severe depression cannot simply will himself out of it. The ill-advised comments only generate more stress and will probably make the person defensive. For example, the statement "What you need is more faith!" will make the person feel worse because it implies that the problem is his own fault. It may even make him feel that God Himself has forsaken him. The presence of emotional or mental problems does not necessarily mean the absence of Christian faith. It may simply be faith under test.

Depression is commonly viewed as a woman's problem, and most attention given to depression is focused on women. But men become just as depressed as women. Whereas women communicate their depression by saying how they feel, men are more likely to act out their feelings. Men tend to become irritable and moody and to withdraw into a little cave. Sometimes they give their loved ones the silent treatment. They mask their depression because they have been taught from boyhood to be tough, that it's silly to cry or admit being hurt. The only thing left is to wear a mask and to hide the feelings that rage within.

Masked depression is a very widespread disorder in the modern world, even though men generally find ways to hide their depressive pain. It is not that the sadness is nonexistent; if you dig deep enough, you will find it present even in our pleasure-mad society. Feelings of depression are shoved out of the way by distracting behaviors, such as anger, arrogance, and bullying. The result is often pain and hardship for the loved ones who must live with the depressed man.

It is most unfortunate that many depressed men, including Christians, will not ask for help to overcome their problems. Some do seek treatment; but even then, a depressed man can be a bear to live with! So what is the best thing to do? Usually the greatest help is someone to stand by—especially a loving, supportive wife. She needs to communicate love and acceptance with all the power she can muster by the grace of God. She must understand that it is better not to ask a depressed man how his day has gone,

THE EMOTIONS

nor is it wise to tell him that the washing machine has been making a strange noise.

God has given men the responsibility of headship, to lead out and to be confident and strong. But when a man becomes depressed, he may go from confidence to frustration, from leading to following, from assurance to doubtfulness. Then his wife must be strong for both herself and her husband, and this reversal of roles may become a great struggle for her. She may find it helpful to recognize that men do not normally choose to be depressed; most of them would gladly give up their depression if they could. God's promise to her is, "My grace is sufficient for thee: for my strength is made perfect in weakness" (2 Corinthians 12:9).

Another struggle may come when the husband does find renewed strength to carry his responsibility; then his wife may find it hard to give his proper role back to him. She may think he is not ready for leadership, but withholding it from him will only add to his old problem. The best thing is to let him take charge even if he makes mistakes; this will do more for him than telling him he is still incompetent. The road to recovery may be lined with both success and failure. Depression usually does not come overnight, nor does it leave in a moment.

As noted before, depression often results from the stress of trying to achieve certain things. If we can master the concept of simply being, we can relax from the compulsion of having to perform at a certain level. This is not to minimize the importance of doing, but to emphasize that *being* is often neglected because *doing* is easier and more noticeable. In other words, do not just try to *do* worthwhile things; stand up and *be* a worthwhile person!

We know that pride is sin; but rather than beating down pride, let us focus on understanding and practicing real humility. It is a false humility that causes us to despise ourselves. True humility includes accepting ourselves as God made us and being deeply grateful for the abilities He has given us. If we do this, we can also rejoice in the abilities and successes of others—and we will not suffer depression for seeming to have less than they.

Discouragement
Probably all of us have experienced the nameless, letdown feeling of emptiness and dejection that discouragement brings. This feeling may follow a spiritual success as well as a spiritual failure. A sense of uncertainty casts a shadow over us and leaves life dangling at loose ends. Are these periods of distress normal for the Christian? If so, are we justified in going through them? Can they be turned into steppingstones in our Christian experience? If they are not normal, what is the best way to deal with them? Let us consider the experiences of some Bible characters for answers to these heart-searching questions.

Moses, Elijah, and Jonah were three great men of God, who became so despondent that they no longer desired to live. Moses said to the Lord, "Kill me, I pray thee, out of hand" (Numbers 11:15). Elijah said, "O LORD, take away my life" (1 Kings 19:4). And Jonah prayed, "O LORD, take, I beseech thee, my life from me" (Jonah 4:3). It is a deep despair indeed that robs a saint of his desire to live, and it must have deep-seated causes.

Moses was a meek man, who achieved great things, and

he bore unbelievable burdens as he brought a rabble of slaves out of Egypt and organized them into a nation. They experienced the miraculous care and provision of God in numerous ways. But the perpetual discontent of the people was so oppressive to Moses that he could no longer endure it. And he besought the Lord to remove him from the scene. He had been driven beyond the limit of his endurance and was overwhelmed with a sense of failure.

The prophet Elijah had just taken part in a spectacular demonstration of God's mighty power. But when he received a death threat from Jezebel, he fled in fear, even though he had so recently defied that woman. It is common for a letdown feeling to follow a great victory or accomplishment. Perhaps we need this to keep us humble and useful. Satan will use such feelings to spoil both the servant and the work of God if we let him.

The city of Nineveh experienced a great revival after Jonah preached there. But instead of leaping for joy over their repentance, Jonah sat brooding outside the city. Why did he become so discouraged? It appears that Jonah's pride was suffering because Nineveh had not been destroyed as he had prophesied.

Why did God not answer these men's requests to die? Consider what would have happened if He had—or if God would take us at our word when we are discouraged. We can be thankful that He knows our frame and declines such requests, for our own good. God usually has something much better than simply removing us from a discouraging situation. Consider Elijah—he went to heaven without experiencing death at all.

Often the greatest temptations of discouragement come

when our condition provides fertile soil for it. Moses' physical endurance had been taxed by the strain of his daily administration. Elijah had gone through the stress of holding a contest at Carmel, praying earnestly for rain, and running thirty miles to Jezreel. Jonah was physically and emotionally spent after his experience in the fish and his witness to the great city of Nineveh. All three men were in a state of physical exhaustion when they succumbed to discouragement.

These three men had demonstrated great zeal for God and jealousy for His cause. But as their emotions drooped, they forgot the spiritual needs of the people and indulged in self-pity. Is not all discouragement and despondency a manifestation of self in one form or another? It is a kind of self-defense for our wounded pride.

Satan likes to use discouragement as a weapon against every person, especially the true child of God. He realizes its potential to bring low even the strongest Christian. Feelings of despondency are not always sin in themselves; but if we dwell on them and live by them, they easily become sin. Discouragement is certainly not an expression of faith, and "whatsoever is not of faith is sin" (Romans 14:23).

Some people seem to think that dwelling in discouragement is part of the Christian life. Joy is associated with pride, they think, so they feel the most "spiritual" when they are discouraged. We do experience distress in connection with trials and tribulations, but discouragement is not on the list of Christian virtues. This sin is often hard to deal with because it is so hard to identify. And when one does label it, he is not sure he wants to get rid of it.

For discouragement can give a kind of religious feeling, and who wants to part with that?

So instead of trying to overcome discouragement, we may feel sorry for ourselves and want others to feel sorry for us too. We may even "cry on the Lord's shoulder" and think we are leaning on His breast as John did at the Last Supper. But we must never nurse discouragement or give it a soft treatment. We need to repent and give it a rude awakening. When we are discouraged, we are of little use to God or anyone else. But God will thoroughly cleanse us from discouragement if we are thorough in dealing with this subtle sin.

What if discouragement arises from a failure in our lives? Then we need to acknowledge our faults, humble ourselves under the mighty hand of God, and let Him bear us up in His everlasting arms. "For a just man falleth seven times, and riseth up again: but the wicked shall fall into mischief [disaster]" (Proverbs 24:16). Jesus said, "Fear not," "Be of good cheer," and "Have faith." May our gaze be more upon Him and less upon ourselves and our situations, and we will be "more than conquerors" over discouragement.

Anger

Anger is a feeling of displeasure about something perceived to be wrong or unjust. It is a basic emotion of the soul—like joy or fear—and as such, it is neither good nor evil of itself. In fact, man would not be man without the ability to become angry. For if we could not become angry, we could not hate and oppose evil. The man who cannot become angry with wrong is lacking in his zeal for right.

The reason that anger is usually wrong is that people so often let it get out of control. Paul wrote, "Be ye angry, and sin not" (Ephesians 4:26). But we do sin if we express anger with loud words and violent actions. We also sin if we become uncommunicative and use the silent treatment. Anger under control can be beneficial; but out of control, it can cause terrible destruction.

You must never grow angry to the point of physical violence. But have you ever become annoyed, frustrated, disappointed, or disgusted with anything? Have you ever been hurt by someone's words? All these feelings are forms of anger—mild forms, to be sure, but anger nevertheless. The best way to deal with these feelings is to recognize them for what they are and to discharge them in constructive ways.

Perhaps we are disturbed by a problem that we see in the church or the school. That feeling of disturbance will motivate us to speak to the responsible persons so that the problem is properly resolved. A key point to remember is that we must deal promptly with anger; for if we bottle it up, it will cause havoc within our souls. "Let not the sun go down upon your wrath" (Ephesians 4:26). If anger is properly discharged, it will bring positive benefits to ourselves and others.

Taking action is not the only constructive way to discharge anger. Many things that we find irritating are so minor that we would do more harm than good in trying to address each one. The person responsible may not even realize that he caused irritation. We should simply pass over such things, as we hope that others will pass over the unintentional annoyances we cause. But it is very important that we consciously forgive the person and dismiss the matter. Otherwise, one irritation may build upon another until finally we vent our accumulated frustration on an innocent person.

Uncontrolled anger is a brief madness. A furious man may think he will lose control of the situation unless he explodes, but his anger actually causes him to lose control of himself. He utters strong, hot words without weighing their meaning or considering how they hurt the victim. He may strike out wildly and do damage far beyond anything he would do in his calmer moments. The words and deeds of anger are over in a moment, but their harm is irrevocable, and their effects continue to work long after the fierce flame of passion has died down.

An outburst of temper is inequitable; there can be no sound judgment when the mind is full of wrathful feelings. An angry man is restricted to only one view of the conduct that enraged him. He sees everything through the mist of his own passions and has no consideration for the ideas or circumstances of those who stirred his anger. How many have injured others and ruined themselves by giving place to wrath!

Since strong feelings of anger make it impossible to reason calmly, the only safe thing to do is to restrain oneself and wait for a more suitable occasion to speak and act. Anger is often more fierce than the occasion demands, and time for reflection will usually moderate it. Such a delay may be crucial in averting disaster. That is why the Bible says, "The discretion of a man deferreth his anger" (Proverbs 19:11).

Deferring anger does not mean that we simply let it

die away. Unresolved anger never expires of its own accord; it continues to smolder in the bosom of a person until he discharges it in some way. He may do this in constructive ways, such as taking proper action or choosing to forgive, as noted above. Or he may use the destructive method of suppressing his anger within himself. Then it becomes a brooding affair that may grow darker and deeper until it turns into full-blown depression. For depression is often a simple case of stifled anger.

Some of us grew up in fairly happy families, where thoughts and emotions were freely aired and tact was almost unheard of. Everyone knew how everyone else felt—whether happy or angry—regardless of whether the others cared to know.

Often the effects of angry outbursts are not fully realized until many years later. By the time we see the harmful results, we may find it very hard to change our habits. Perhaps we have even become addicted to anger because of the way it releases tensions. We may think we need to let off steam in order to feel better again. But we must realize that losing our tempers is always wrong, and we need to make it right if that happens.

With God's help and a better understanding, we can recognize our anger problem and deal constructively with it. One big step is simply to know the facts about anger: that the feelings in themselves are not wrong, and that they can actually be useful if we carefully control them. Another step is to care more about the effect of anger on our loved ones than about its benefit to ourselves. This application of the Golden Rule will work wonders in helping us to control our tempers.

Anger may be in order as a protest against sin and injustice, but it must never do wrong to others. Neither must it mete out vengeance and retribution, which belong to God alone. May we never answer an angry word with an angry word, for it is the second one that usually causes the quarrel. He who loses his temper in any discussion is always wrong—even if he is right.

"My beloved brethren, let every man be swift to hear, slow to speak, slow to wrath: for the wrath of man worketh not the righteousness of God" (James 1:19, 20). Things done in uncontrolled anger will not further but will rather hinder the work of God and His church. Love is the power that wins men's hearts and draws them together. Love will make us "more than conquerors" over the wrath of man.

Resentment

Of all the things that hinder spiritual growth, resentment is one of the most effective. We are made for love, and to assimilate love and hate at the same time is impossible. For resentment is a form of hatred, a settled anger against someone because of a real or an imagined injustice. A sudden flare-up of anger is bad enough, but slow-burning resentment is devastating both spiritually and physically.

Resentment may develop after a misfortune, such as a physical injury or a financial loss. If we brood over our "unfair" situation, we can get into a state of self-pity that is even worse than the initial loss. Or perhaps we think others have much better financial opportunities than we ever had, and we develop a resentful spirit because of it.

"More Than Conquerors"

The attitude that "nothing ever works in my favor" and "everyone is against me" may be the very thing that causes us go bankrupt, both literally and spiritually.

Resentment causes our whole physical and mental system to operate on the basis of war rather than peace. Living with a war mentality is a constant drain on our being. We cannot think straight if we hold resentment, for everything is distorted and biased. Resentment not only dims the spiritual vision and obscures the inner life; it can even make things look darker physically.

If a rattlesnake is cornered, it may become so frenzied that it bites itself. We do something similar when we harbor resentment; we actually bite ourselves. For if resentment is dropped into the subconscious mind and the lid is shut, it will wreak havoc within our souls. We may have a reason for our resentment; but with or without a reason, it will be destructive to our souls and bodies. It will consume us and burn us out. Someone may say, "He burns me up"—and that is altogether true. Resentment is always more destructive to ourselves than to its object.

Resentment follows different channels in different stages of life. Young people tend to resent being counseled by those who are older, when the experiences of their elders could be of great value to their success and welfare. Indeed, a young person (or an older one) sometimes holds a long and cancerous resentment against a person who sincerely offered him some timely and needful advice. Such an attitude may rise not only against advice but also against a superior example of Christian conduct. May we never be so foolish that we let resentment rob us of the blessing of wise counsel from those who truly love us.

The Emotions

Some people in middle age, especially women, become resentful because they feel unwanted and unneeded. Perhaps their children have grown up and left home, and their husbands are absorbed in business. Or the middle-aged man may be expecting a long-awaited job promotion, but he sees a younger man put ahead of him. Something similar may even happen in church life when a younger brother is assigned to a position that we had expected to fill. We may consider ourselves better qualified and may even have more time to give to the cause. Many have disqualified themselves even after long years of service simply because they allowed resentment to take control of their lives.

How can we free ourselves from the chains of resentment? The apostle Paul wrote, "Be ye angry, and sin not: let not the sun go down upon your wrath: neither give place to the devil" (Ephesians 4:26, 27). This suggests that if we hold on to anger, sleep over it, let it turn into resentment—we are giving the devil room to work. Never let that happen! Do not hang on to resentment and justify it by calling it righteous indignation. Settle in your mind the fact that all resentment is wrong, no matter how well justified. A resentful spirit is totally at variance with the Christian law of love. If your anger is truly justified, turn it into a burden of prayer before God.

Surrender all resentment to God, and consent for Him to take it away. Yes, you have been hurt; tell God all about it, and seek His enabling grace to rise above it. He alone can heal your wounded spirit and soul and give you peace and calmness in its place. Then actively forgive anyone against whom you have held resentment.

Each time the person's name comes to your mind, breathe a prayer for him. Try to do good to the person; be gracious and redemptive.

Love people for what they can become, not for what they are or what they have done to you. If a relationship suddenly breaks down, get into the habit of settling things at once. Do not let discord become cold and fixed in thought and attitude. Jesus said, "Agree with thine adversary quickly." Refuse to be offended by any offense from others, whether great or small. When you are filled with the love of God, there is no room for resentment in your heart.

Love is immortal; it is of God. Love is the end to which all other graces are the means. Love is the bond of perfectness. It is supreme; love alone can overcome hatred, malice, and ill will. Love will make us "more than conquerors" over resentment, through the grace of Christ, who Himself overcame all the evils of the human heart and soul.

Bitterness

"Follow peace with all men, and holiness, without which no man shall see the Lord: looking diligently lest any man fail of the grace of God; lest any root of bitterness springing up trouble you, and thereby many be defiled" (Hebrews 12:14, 15).

This passage indicates that once we lose the grace of God, a root of bitterness may begin growing downward and springing upward. A root is an apt picture of bitterness, for both work underground, out of sight, and both bear fruit of one kind or another. Bitterness grows out of conflict, and that conflict often develops an extensive

THE EMOTIONS

growth underground before we see any visible signs on the surface. We tend not to tell others about our inner conflicts. We keep them hidden to protect ourselves against the invasion of anyone else. The grace of God could help us, but we have lost it for one reason or another.

If anyone mentions bitterness, we deny it immediately. "I don't hold bitterness; I have forgiven!" But to deny what is there will only aggravate the problem. The bitterness will continue to grow and to trouble us; and the more we try to justify it, the worse it will become. Yet we continue to tell ourselves and others, "I am not bitter; I'm hurt—just hurt!"

This underground bitterness cannot always stay hidden as a root; it will finally come forth and bear fruit. The fruits of bitterness are many and varied: complaining, blaming, self-pity, shifting of responsibility, rebellious anger, and others. These fruits have different forms, but they all have the same bitter flavor.

Complaining. Bitterness leads to complaining because things are not right within us; therefore nothing seems right around us. We become discontent and complain about our circumstances, the faults of others, and even the weather. The real problem is not these outward things but our own inner guilt and discontent. Complaining only adds to the bitterness and dissatisfaction in our souls.

Blaming. A person who complains will soon be finding fault with others and blaming them for one misdeed or another. The blame may come directly, in the form of unsparing accusations; or it may come indirectly, in the form of polite words loaded with sarcasm, insinuations, and hidden meanings. Why do people so readily blame others? They are using blame to balance the scales, to offset their own guilt by calling attention to the faults of others. They do not feel so bad about their own failures if they can prove that others are guilty too.

Some people carry on their shoulders a whole sack of charges against their friends and neighbors. They say they want help with their problems, but then they take down their sack and show what all is in it. These problems are not their own but those of other people. For example, the schoolteacher said this or did that. The ministers said or did the wrong thing, or they failed to do what they should have done. The church is wrong in doing this or requiring that. And on and on they go, displaying their accumulated treasures of bitterness and ill feelings.

Collecting treasures of blame is a far cry from laying up treasures in heaven! Such blaming is wrong because of what it does to ourselves and others. As long as I point a finger at someone else, I am not repenting of my own sin. As long as I am blaming my neighbor, I have no chance of truly helping him. Blaming also violates the two greatest commandments, which tell us to love God with all our hearts and to love our neighbors as ourselves. These blaming people do not want help but sympathy. They want you to agree that they are right and that everyone else is wrong.

A natural illustration will show how this process often works. Suppose John wants me to come over and help him fix his lawn mower. In the process, John does something that causes the blade to cut my hand. Now do I just forget about it? No; I go inside and wash it carefully to make sure all the dirt is out. Then I bandage it up and go back out to John, who apologizes for his carelessness. I tell him

The Emotions

it's all right; I know he didn't do it on purpose.

The next day, I meet some friends and want to show them my injury. So I open the thing up and let them see how sore it is. The day after that, I do the same thing for some more of my friends; and the third day, I open it and show it to still others. Am I helping the wound to heal? Certainly not; I am only making the matter worse and getting dirt into it every time I open it.

About the fourth day, I see a streak going up my arm. Oh, the cut is infected! I must see a doctor, or I may get blood poisoning and even lose my arm. So I go to the doctor and tell him all about how it was hurt. "You see, John did it; it wasn't my fault. It was his carelessness, not mine." When I get the doctor bill, I think John should feel responsible to pay it.

Now I tell my friends how the whole thing happened and how high the doctor bill is. "Don't you think John should take care of that? All the suffering I've lived with is enough; he should pay the bill." When my friends try to tell me it would have healed if I hadn't opened it so often, I say, "Oh, no, you don't understand. I just wanted you to know how much it hurt and that it was John's fault, not mine." My wound has become a kind of security for me; if it heals, I won't have anything to talk about. The spiritual parallel is far too common among professing Christians.

Self-pity. A self-pitying person feels that no one appreciates him and that everyone is against him. This may seem like low self-esteem, but it is actually a high opinion of oneself. "See how much I've suffered, and nobody even cares. I don't deserve anything like this!" Self-pity is consoling for the moment but crushing in the end. It binds a person to his own stake of self-martyrdom. He may clearly demonstrate a bitter spirit while constantly saying he is not bitter about anything.

Shifting of responsibility. A bitter person is never the one at fault. "I did what I did because of what you did. If you hadn't become angry, I wouldn't have lost my temper. You started the argument; I only tried to end it." This shifting of responsibility is as old as the Garden of Eden, where Adam blamed Eve and Eve blamed the serpent. Adam even tried to shift the responsibility back on God.

Rebellious anger. A bitter person may develop such feelings of frustration that he frequently lashes out at people around him. This may bother him at first, but eventually it develops into a natural response, a habit of exploding whenever he is overcome by strong emotions. Each time he vents his anger, resentment, and bitterness, it becomes easier to do it again. Self-expression may become such a way of life that he hardly even tries to control himself anymore.

People who stay bitter for a long time develop illusory and warped thinking patterns. They can turn the most loving words and actions of other people into offenses. They can change truth into lying, love into hate, and good into evil. What tremendous power is in a root of bitterness, and what trouble and defilement it can bring!

What is God's way of deliverance from bitterness? First, we must acknowledge that we have a problem, and we must truly want deliverance. We need to repent of our spiteful feelings and actions; they are our fault and no one else's. God's solution is to love, not hate; to forgive, not hold grudges; to repent, not take our own way. We may not feel like loving and forgiving; we may not like to give up our comfortable habits; but let us do it anyway. It is the best therapy we can give ourselves, for it is God's way, and it will bring deliverance and perfect rest.

Tension

Why are we often tense? It is because we are not sure that God is backing us, and we feel the need to stand on our own. We may not be full of fears and anxieties, but we are tense and exhausted. We need to learn the art of relaxing and receiving, or we will drive our conscious and subconscious mind to work overtime, even a twenty-four-hour shift.

Tension is like a rocking chair; it gives us something to do, but it never gets us anywhere. Even worse, it will wear us out while going nowhere. Tension may be beneficial when it is properly harnessed to meet an emergency; but when it is out of control, it will leave us defeated and burned out.

Christian faith teaches us to rest and be calm as we wait on God and follow His revealed will. We need true faith in God for all areas of the Christian life, even the areas that are not clearly spelled out. For example, the uncertainty involved in making a major choice, especially that of choosing a life companion, may cause so much tension that it actually disqualifies a person from making that choice. However, even a deep disappointment may be turned into a useful purpose if we simply rest in God's provision for us.

Parents may become tense because of their children's choice of marriage partners. This may be a consequence of neglect in giving proper guidance to their children while they were very young. If we place education, wealth, and social status above Christian character, we set ourselves up for the tension that comes when children choose life companions who have little appreciation for our Christian values. Such a tension will affect not only us as parents but also the lives of our children and their families.

Many homes experience tension because of a tight daily schedule. As our activities increase, we may feel that we are accomplishing more than our forebears; but in the final analysis, are we as successful as we think? What we call success may pay dividends in broken-down communications between husband and wife and between parents and children, which can only add to the tension and stress in a family. Tension may set in for reasons other than having a tight schedule, and it will not stop within the confines of our homes. Our tension at home will reveal itself in our communications with the outside world and certainly in our church relationships.

Sometimes we experience tension because of a false sense of duty. We may feel we are indispensable and blame ourselves if something does not work as planned. We should feel responsible for our assigned duties, but to be under tension while fulfilling them will only make the load heavier and will hinder our effectiveness. Setting deadlines for accomplishments may be rewarding, but it may also cause unnecessary tension and strain.

Tension may develop simply because we have adopted

THE EMOTIONS

the fast tempo of modern life. We think we are not performing well unless we are doing things in a hurry. The Lord may need to allow things that slow us down, because we are going too fast; and since He knows our frame, He often does this even before we sense the need of it. Let us not allow such "hindrances" to increase our tension, for God knows what is best for us.

Life is too short and precious to have it tied up in knots of tension and frustration. The real reason for these problems lies too often in an unsurrendered will. May we humbly say, "Lord, not my will; only Your will be done. The burdens of life are too great for me. I give them all to You, for I am not strong enough to carry them myself." This is the secret of being "more than conquerors" over tension, for God has all power over life, time, and circumstances.

Part 3

The Body of Man

CHAPTER 8

The Physical Body

We have seen that the spirit has the three faculties of intuition, communion, and conscience, and the soul has the three faculties of will, mind, and emotions. The body is the outer shell, where the spirit and soul reside, and it likewise has three parts: flesh, blood, and bones. The flesh is the soft tissue of the body, the blood is the fluid wherein is the life of the body, and the bones are the hard structures that give form to the body.

Because the physical senses are found in the body, the meaning of *body* or *flesh* is extended to describe the sensual nature of man. This nature is depraved and prone to sin; it is weak, low, and bent toward ungodliness and vice. It is sold under sin, and within it dwells no good thing (see Romans 7:18). Apart from God's power operating through the spirit and soul, the body is incapable of producing anything but sin in its drive for self-gratification.

Whereas the spirit and soul of man are regenerated by the new birth, the body is not changed. It must be brought into subjection to the spirit and soul through the power of the Holy Spirit. But the devil constantly appeals to man through his sensual appetites to entice him to sin. This is Satan's primary avenue of approach, whereas God works through man's spirit. The ungodly man lives to satisfy the dictates of his body, but the godly man lives to follow the Spirit's directives as He sanctifies the soul and body.

"What? know ye not that your body is the temple of the Holy Ghost which is in you, which ye have of God, and ye are not your own?" (1 Corinthians 6:19). The apostle might have said that God's Spirit dwells in our spirits, which is true. But our bodies are the physical temples where our spirits and the Holy Spirit dwell together. That is why the body must be sanctified; the Holy Spirit will not dwell in an unholy temple.

Paul wrote elsewhere that he was weak in body, but the power of Christ made him strong. How did that work? It was through the life of Christ exhibited in Paul's mortal flesh. This means he received grace to endure pain, and resurrection power to perform physical tasks so strenuous that they might have been impossible otherwise. Paul experienced in a literal sense the truth of Christ's words: "My grace is sufficient for thee: for my strength is made perfect in weakness."

God also gives us physical strength, but not to be used for our own pleasure. Right here is reason enough why our prayers for health and strength are sometimes unanswered. Do we ask for these blessings just so that we may live in comfort and convenience? It is normal to desire strong, healthy bodies with as little pain as possible, but that may not fulfill God's highest purposes. We should simply accept the strength that He provides and never question why we are not as strong and healthy as others may be.

"For if ye live after the flesh, ye shall die: but if ye through

The Physical Body

the Spirit do mortify the deeds of the body, ye shall live" (Romans 8:13). This verse describes the proper relationship of the believer to the Holy Spirit and to his body. But some professing Christians act like two different people. Sometimes they are tuned to the desires of the inner man; then they feel spiritual and close to God and full of life. But at other times they are tuned to the desires of the flesh; then they feel fallen and carnal and alienated from God. Such people often have little toleration for physical discomfort. Any slight pain or illness will disquiet them and make them miserable. It is impossible to follow a spiritual course if we live like this.

Some may say, "There is nothing wrong with fulfilling legitimate desires of the flesh." That is true to a point, but God says through His Word and Spirit that the flesh will profit us nothing and that we owe it nothing. We do need food, clothing, and shelter for our bodies, along with rest and exercise. Yet these necessities must never become the main objective in life. Sometimes we must override our basic needs for the sake of God and His kingdom. For example, fasting may be more needful than feasting when we seek special direction or blessing from God in a specific situation. If we live by the flesh, we will die even while we make every effort to stay alive and well. But if we live by the Spirit, we will live even while our mortal bodies are fast declining.

God wants us to take care of our bodies, but He does not want us to care more about our physical welfare than about our spiritual relationship with Him. Neither is God pleased when we become so engrossed with the symptoms of illness that we look away from Him and seek help outside of His healing hand. When sickness comes, can we accept it as something that God permitted and let Him provide healing as He will? Or will we search for healing whether or not a quick cure is God's will?

We must be careful to maintain a balance on this point. Even though God wants us to trust Him for health and healing, He expects us to use common sense in keeping our bodies healthy. We need to give attention to proper diet, exercise, and rest. However, God sometimes wants to show us that medical science and good hygiene cannot guarantee physical health. If we have good health, it is ultimately a gift from God and not a product of our own achievement.

Man Is Flesh

"And the LORD said, My spirit shall not always strive with man, for that he also is flesh: yet his days shall be an hundred and twenty years" (Genesis 6:3). God's statement that man is flesh suggests that degenerate man is much like the animals, driven by the appetites of his body. His spirit and soul do not rule his body but are ruled by it. This allows Satan to take control of man by working through his senses, which are the driving forces of his life. In this way, Satan establishes his power over man, in opposition to God's authority.

Jesus said something similar when He told Nicodemus, "That which is born of the flesh is flesh" (John 3:6). Everything that a man inherits physically from his parents belongs to the flesh. Man does not become fleshly by a gradual process of sinning until finally his whole being is controlled by the carnal passions. He is fleshly as soon as he is born.

The Physical Body

All men by birth are carnal, immoral, and sold under sin. There is no exception and no distinction. All men are born equally depraved, bent on satisfying their own evil nature. No amount of education, improvement, cultivation, morality, or religious devotion can change this fact. No power under heaven can convert or alter the sinful nature.

Unregenerate man may desire the will of God with his mind and determine to do it with all the power of his will. But these actions of the soul are no match for the flesh, which is exceeding strong in following carnal passions. "For to will is present with me; but how to perform that which is good I find not" (Romans 7:18). Man has no power in himself to do good consistently, no matter how strongly he may desire it. He has no hope of becoming righteous on his own.

The only recourse is for man to receive a new nature and gain strength greater than that of the carnal nature. The flesh must be overpowered and conquered so completely that for all practical purposes it is dead. "Reckon ye also yourselves to be dead indeed unto sin, but alive unto God through Jesus Christ our Lord" (Romans 6:11). How is this possible? The answer lies in the crucifixion of Christ.

When Jesus was crucified, He was made a sin offering for us (see 2 Corinthians 5:21). Without becoming sinful Himself, Jesus became the representative of sin and received the penalty for sin, which is death. When Jesus died on the cross and rose again, the power of sin over human flesh was broken. Now as we choose by faith to be crucified with Him, sin is rendered powerless to dominate us. The strength of the carnal nature is broken, and we are free to serve God!

One point must be kept clear. It is a gross error to think that once we are joined with Christ in His death, our carnal nature is annihilated or eradicated. The old nature will remain within us as long as we live, as evil and depraved as ever. Whether saint or sinner, the flesh is the same; it is not transformed by regeneration. The difference comes only as God works new life and power in the spirit and soul, and the flesh comes into subjection to this higher authority. The flesh is still very much alive, but it is dead in that it has no freedom to carry out its desires.

Regeneration is the beginning of new spiritual life in Christ. But this new life does not mean that we will cease to have temptations and conflicts. Satan does not give up without a hard struggle. In fact, conflicts may increase, not only because Satan and self are dethroned but also because sin is deeply rooted in our flesh. After all, the flesh has found pleasure in sin for a long time. But we do not need to have an intense, protracted struggle that includes repeatedly indulging in sin. Such an experience would indicate that we do not have a real hatred for sin.

When those who are young in the faith are assailed by these conflicts, it can bring them almost to despair. They may wonder if they are truly saved. Remember that regeneration in itself brings on the struggle. When the flesh was in authority, we could sin and feel little sense of sinfulness. Now that new life and heavenly desires have come, sin appears exceeding sinful. "The flesh lusteth against the Spirit, and the Spirit against the flesh," each seeking to overpower the other. This battle may be distressing at times, but it does confirm that we have been regenerated and that God is working in us through His Spirit.

Through Jesus Christ, we can be "more than conquerors" in the struggle against sin. We must yield our whole spirit, soul, and body to His dominion. Then when He returns, we will be delivered from our sinful flesh to enjoy "the glorious liberty of the children of God" (Romans 8:21).

The Flesh Crucified

We have observed that Satan works through the flesh, including the five senses, to defile the body, soul, and spirit of man. The only way to be delivered from this process is through the work of Christ on the cross. What we want to see now is how Satan works through the flesh of a believer to gain access to his soul and spirit. For Satan does not willingly give up one of his subjects; he will do all he can to bring the believer back under his power.

The works of the flesh are of two kinds: the fulfilling of unlawful desires (lusts), and the performing of good deeds to give an appearance of righteousness (self-righteousness). There is no question that the works of the flesh, such as hatred, theft, and fornication, are defiling sins. But hypocrisy and self-righteousness are also works of the flesh—*and they are just as defiling as the sins of lust.* Hypocrisy in particular is abhorrent to Christ; just read His denunciations of the scribes and Pharisees in Matthew 23.

What is the difference between true righteousness and self-righteousness? True righteousness is performed in the power of God for the glory of God. Self-righteousness is performed in the power of the flesh for the glory of self. The motivation behind every action is self-gratification. Self opposes the Spirit of God and thwarts His work by operating in its own power instead of relying on the grace of God.

The thing that deceives many believers is that the flesh can do so many good things. But the fact that it is actively doing good is proof that it is still alive and in control. Indeed, there are many who have high moral standards; they may do notable deeds of charity and even give thousands of dollars to humanitarian causes. But too often, these things are done for self-glory rather than God's glory. To prove this, consider what happens when a respected person is falsely accused of scandalous conduct. Almost certainly, he will become bitter, and his "high morals" may even fall suddenly by the wayside.

Right here lies the error that some believers make: they see only the evil in the flesh and fail to see that the flesh can produce an excellent imitation of true righteousness. We must see fleshly works as works of the flesh, whether they are clearly evil or whether they appear to be good. For if the believer lets his good works come from the flesh, he will soon find himself working evil. This is Satan's way of gaining access to the soul. Self-righteousness leads inevitably to gross unrighteousness.

Good deeds of the flesh are performed without dependence on the Holy Spirit, without an attitude of obedience to Christ, without a spirit of humility, and without praying and waiting upon God. Such deeds will bring deception and delusion because we think we are serving God when we are actually serving ourselves. Jesus said, "For

I say unto you, That except your righteousness shall exceed the righteousness of the scribes and Pharisees, ye shall in no case enter into the kingdom of heaven" (Matthew 5:20). Any good that comes from self is an abomination to God because it does not proceed from the Spirit and life of Christ.

Satan wants us to blend our own goodness with the goodness that comes through faith in Christ. This is similar to what the believers at Galatia were doing. Paul wrote, "Are ye so foolish? having begun in the Spirit, are ye now made perfect by the flesh?" (Galatians 3:3). The Galatians began in the power of the Spirit, but then they tried to perfect their righteousness with good works of their own doing. The same temptation comes to all believers. But there is no salvation and no righteousness apart from the power of Jesus Christ. As no one can save himself by his own efforts, so no one can perfect himself by his own good works.

We must operate by the rule of "no confidence in the flesh." One who has self-confidence reposes in his own wisdom. He may be able to hear and believe the Word; to read and preach the Bible; but all is executed in the power of the flesh and not the Holy Spirit. Jesus said, "This people draweth nigh unto me with their mouth, and honoureth me with their lips; but their heart is far from me" (Matthew 15:8). A man may speak profound spiritual truths and still be as fleshly as one who makes no profession of religion.

Why is it that some believers eagerly seek a wholly consecrated life, but fail time and again? They have tasted the sweetness of an abundant life in Christ and desire to continue into greater depths of maturity. But, alas, how quickly it vanishes, and again they struggle to find that sweet repose. Why do they so soon lose the lofty experience, and how can they be restored? The answer is clear and unmistakable. They are trusting in the flesh to do what was begun in the Spirit. They are substituting carnal power for Spirit power.

Such people are themselves leading the way, hoping the Holy Spirit will come alongside and give assistance. When they pray, "Lord, help us to live holy lives," or "Help us not to sin against You," they seem to be saying that they can get along fairly well except in the more difficult decisions and temptations. This may be a startling thought, but is it not the experience of far too many of God's children?

The good works of the flesh seem so close to God's way of righteousness that a believer may think that they are the moving of God's Spirit. So satisfying is the experience that his emotions and will may also be deceived. There may even be a degree of success in overcoming certain temptations. Yet the person fails to sense a complete, assuring victory over besetting sins. Why all this frustration? Is it normal to experience such uncertainty? The answer lies in whether the believer is depending on God for victory or is exerting his own righteousness.

If the flesh is not allowed to give expression to sin, it will consent to do good. It does this so that it can revert to sin at the first opportunity. Satan knows how to manipulate the flesh to gain his ends. He knows full well that if he can keep the good side of the flesh in action, he has a base from which to operate and to recover what was lost through regeneration. If he can get the believer to have victory over certain sins in the power of the flesh, he has a good chance of alienating him from the Holy Spirit and eventually causing him to lose his faith in God. This is one reason that some believers fall back into sin after they have been set free.

How can the believer see his flesh as God sees it? God may allow him to become weak and even fall into sin so that he may understand that no good resides in his flesh. Sometimes God permits Satan to attack him so that out of his suffering and defeat he may perceive the truth about his flesh. These lessons may be most difficult and are not learned in one day or night. The believer may even go through a long, bitter struggle, perhaps like that described in Romans 7, before he finally realizes that he cannot put confidence in his flesh.

God's will can never be accomplished in us until our flesh is denied and crucified. This means laying down all pride, all self-exaltation, all desire for honor and recognition. It means humbly bearing the reproach of Christ and willingly suffering for His sake. There must be a complete committal of the flesh to the cross and a total yielding to the Holy Spirit. "I am crucified with Christ: nevertheless I live; yet not I, but Christ liveth in me: and the life which I now live in the flesh I live by the faith of the Son of God, who loved me, and gave himself for me" (Galatians 2:20).

The crucifying of the flesh is an ongoing operation; it is not a one-time experience that puts the flesh permanently out of power. Let us not be deceived into thinking that we can have an experience by which the flesh has no more power to entice and ruin us. Neither let us believe

Satan's lie that we are eternally secure in Christ and cannot go back to serving the flesh anymore. Such deception will be the very means by which we return to living after the flesh.

Death to the flesh comes by choosing that Christ will live His life in us. We must constantly abide in this: death to the flesh, and resurrected life to the soul and spirit by the power of the Holy Spirit. Herein lies our only security. Herein lies the power to be "more than conquerors" through Christ, who loved us and gave His entire self for us.

Temptation

All men are subject to temptation. It comes in all ages to the great and good as well as to the ordinary and sinful. The conditions of our life on earth make temptation unavoidable. Since God gave man the power of moral choice, it must be that man should face circumstances that compel him to decide between good and evil. And since we live in a probationary state, we must confront temptations to prove whether we are on God's side or the devil's.

Becoming a Christian does not exempt one from temptation. Conversion never alters a man's circumstances; it only alters his relation to the circumstances. But the Christian from his loftier position can see virtue wrung from the enticements of the tempter. Temptation may even take a more subtle and perilous form for the Christian. He may discover temptations that less perceptive souls fail to recognize.

Some sensitive people think they must be very sinful because they are tempted so much. But a multiplicity of temptations is often an evidence of faithfulness and integrity. The strongest attacks are made upon the strongest forts. Satan would not be so earnestly seeking to capture us if we were already in his power. Repeated temptation speaks of steadfast opposition; and as long we resist temptation, we do not sin.

Some dread temptation because they think it will force them to do evil. But since the world began, no man has ever been compelled to commit a single sin. Satan has no power of compulsion. Actually, being compelled to sin is a contradiction of terms, for what is done under compulsion is not sin. Temptation at its strongest is only inducement; we do not sin until we choose to yield.

This does not mean that we can overcome temptation in our own strength. Because of our evil nature, we simply do not have the power to resist temptation. So we must enter into a covenant with God through Christ and trust in His power to keep us from falling.

God regulates temptation according to the bearing power of the one who is tempted. He "will not suffer you to be tempted above that ye are able" (1 Corinthians 10:13). His voice says, "So far and no further," even as when Job was tempted (see Job 1:12; 2:6). God does even more; He "will with the temptation also make a way to escape, that ye may be able to bear it." Note this great truth: *Every temptation is accompanied with a way of escape.* The temptation and the escape are always joined and can never be parted. What a marvelous provision!

Jesus Christ Himself was tempted while He lived on earth. He came in a body like that of Adam's in his innocence, to be tempted as Adam was. Though Christ was free from the drag of a fallen nature, that did not exempt

Him from the possibility of falling into sin. Adam's and Christ's temptations came wholly from without, and they appealed to inward desires that were wholly innocent. Both Adam and Christ had volitional power to yield or not to yield to temptation. Adam yielded, but Christ was victorious; His character remained perfectly flawless.

Our Lord was genuinely human even in His sinlessness; that attribute did not in itself exclude the possibility of sinning. If Christ could not have fallen, His sinlessness would have little meaning. But having been exposed to the severest temptations and having triumphed over them all, His sinlessness is glorious as never before. His victory was not in *being not able to sin,* but in *being able not to sin.* That same victory can be ours through His power.

Jesus' temptations in the wilderness are a mirror of the temptations we face. Satan's first appeal to Jesus was that of satisfying a bodily desire, which was the same way he had tempted Eve. Appealing to the body is always Satan's first avenue of approach. He knows that if he gains power over man's body, he can gain access to his soul and spirit as well.

When Satan tempted Jesus to turn stones into bread, Jesus did not challenge him with reason. He turned instead to the authority of the Scriptures. "It is written, Man shall not live by bread alone, but by every word that proceedeth out of the mouth of God." Jesus had memorized many Scripture passages, which is something we must do if we hope to resist temptation. Jesus also had His values right. As important as natural food is, it is wrong even to feed the body if that violates God's words

The Physical Body

(in this case, by trusting in His own powers for physical sustenance). Thus Jesus overcame the temptation that came through His flesh.

Satan then tempted Jesus by taking Him to the pinnacle of the temple and quoting Scripture himself. "If thou be the Son of God, cast thyself down: for it is written, He shall give his angels charge concerning thee: and in their hands they shall bear thee up, lest at any time thou dash thy foot against a stone." This temptation was at the opposite extreme from the first one. The first temptation was that of distrust; the second was that of rash overconfidence, or presumption. But though Satan could tempt Jesus to jump from the top of the pinnacle, he could not push Him off.

In the second temptation, Satan shifted from making an appeal to the flesh to making an appeal to the soul. This was a temptation to lift up the soul, to make a grand display of self for personal advantage. So Satan tempts people today to seek power and greatness in the eyes of men, to exalt self at the expense of glorifying God alone.

Jesus responded by saying, "It is written again, Thou shalt not tempt the Lord thy God." To trust God in unavoidable dangers is faith; to tempt God by putting oneself in obvious danger is presumption. Jesus' power to perform miracles was not intended for vain display but for revealing God's great plan of redemption to mankind. His miracles were wrought to relieve distress and increase the faith of His followers, not merely to startle and amaze people.

In Christ's third temptation, the devil took Jesus "up into an exceeding high mountain, and sheweth him all the kingdoms of the world, and the glory of them; and saith unto him, All these things will I give thee, if thou wilt fall down and worship me." Since the third temptation involved worship, it was an appeal to the spirit. It must have been a tempting prospect, for Jesus had come to be King. Now Satan was offering an easy way to get a worldwide kingdom—without the dreadful shame and suffering of the cross.

Jesus might have reasoned that the end justifies the means, but He answered Satan with prompt and absolute decisiveness. "Get thee hence, Satan: for it is written, Thou shalt worship the Lord thy God, and him only shalt thou serve." Jesus lost no time in pondering over or playing with the temptation. He did not even rebuke Satan for his arrogance in wanting to be worshiped. Jesus simply referred to the command that we are to worship God and Him alone. This simple, direct approach is a vital key for overcoming temptation.

Let us take a few more lessons from this experience of Jesus. The Spirit may lead us into a place where we are tempted, but He never tempts us to sin. Every individual is personally responsible for his own sin. But as in Jesus' case, God provides grace to endure temptation, and He sends comfort and sustenance afterward. We are not tempted in order to be ruined but to be made strong. Actually, every temptation is an opportunity for getting closer to God; it gives an occasion to cast ourselves in humble dependence upon Him.

Through Christ, we can be "more than conquerors" over the temptations of Satan. Because Jesus was victorious over all sin, temptation has no claim upon us. We are free by His power—free to do the will of God, free to yield our members to Him in righteousness and holiness. Someday we shall have immortal bodies that will be eternally free from temptation and sin. What a glorious prospect!

Feelings of Infirmity

Jesus was "touched with the feeling of our infirmities [weaknesses]" and "was in all points tempted like as we are, yet without sin" (Hebrews 4:15). He was truly and fully divine as well as truly and fully human. We need to accept this double truth by faith, or we will not be able to avail ourselves of the vast spiritual resources in Christ.

In order for Jesus to identify with us, He needed to become human like His brethren. Part of being human is to have limitations, which often bring feelings of weakness and inadequacy. Some people can hardly live with their weaknesses; and as a result, they find it hard to accept their humanity. But Jesus was not ashamed of being human! As we see Him walking through the Gospels, we feel the love and approval of the Father for His Son. Knowing that Christ fully accepted His humanity will help to free us to live our own human lives.

We tend to be afraid of revealing who we really are. We fear that if we expose our true selves, others may reject us because they do not like what they see. But to be truly human and fully functioning, we must overcome this fear and let other people see our real selves, including our inner feelings. Do we live a double life? Is our public life different from our private life? Are we playing a role that is different from what we really are?

Take, for instance, the common greeting, "How are

you?" Do you respond out of your true self or through a mask? Suppose you have had a rough week, your family is in a mild crisis, or you have a nagging cold or a bad headache. To answer out of your true self, you would need to share some of these feelings with the other person. But most likely, you will respond through your mask and say, "I'm fine, thank you. How are you?" We are expected to have everything under control at all times and to be pleasant and cheerful. We don't like to hear others complain, so we excuse ourselves by thinking that the other person doesn't really want to know how we feel anyway. If we do tell him, he may brand us as a complainer—and we do not want that!

Every person has a role to fill, and he is constantly picking up signals that describe the proper way to fill that role. The businessman must be a driving, creative person. The scientist tends to be cold and impersonal. The officer must take a tough, authoritative stance. Nurses are always compassionate with all patients. Clergymen should appear pious at all times. But are we compelled to keep up the image at all costs? What do we have to lose if we must say "I made a mistake" or "I don't know" or "I'm not able to do that"? We can become so taken up with wearing masks that our spiritual lives get tied up in knots.

The greater the difference between what is expected of us and what we really are, the greater our inner stress. Some people feel so compelled to constantly keep up a front that they never let themselves be their true selves. Why not simply admit to the coming and going of doubts or dilemmas or dry spells in our spiritual lives? If we can acknowledge the real truth about ourselves, we will be on

THE PHYSICAL BODY

the road to victory by the power and grace of Christ.

Many of us are afraid of our feelings. They are strange creatures that we do not understand or know what to do with, which run seemingly at random from dark despair to the heights of ecstasy. We have little control over our feelings, with the result that we become embarrassed about our actions and reactions. If we feel the pain of depression or grief and openly express that feeling by weeping, we fear that others will think us childish or lacking in self-control. We therefore suppress our God-given feelings, which is a most unfortunate thing. The price may be emotional and spiritual breakdown.

Strong feelings have a charge of emotional energy, and no person can dispel that charge simply by denying or repressing the feelings. You do not get rid of the emotional charge of anger by refusing to admit that you are angry and smiling pleasantly instead. You only drive the emotional charge within yourself, where it can cause serious trouble down the road.

Of course, there are proper and improper ways to express feelings. Some ways are healthy and constructive, while others are unhealthy and even destructive. A child deserves to see feelings expressed in appropriate ways. He will learn to properly express joy, anger, and sorrow if his parents set a good example. But if parents suppress their own feelings and forbid the child to express his, the child will experience inner turmoil, which has many adverse effects.

Feelings can be expressed in two ways: by impulse or by calm deliberation. Both will satisfy our need for expression, but expressing a feeling by impulse will seldom have positive results. Impulsive people often completely bypass personal restraint. They just let it loose with little regard for the surroundings or the situation. A calm, rational expression of feelings will discharge the emotional energy while avoiding the harm done by expressing feelings impulsively or by suppressing them.

Some may think traditional Christian worship suppresses normal feelings. But worship in the Christian church should be characterized by dignity and solemnity. The atmosphere should be quiet, the mood serious, the hymns sung earnestly, and the Communion observed reverently. There is no air of gloom in all this, but an expression of the worshipers' deepest and truest feelings. A worship service held with propriety does not need to degenerate into formality. Formality is cold and unexpressive of people's feelings.

Christians are faced with feelings of disappointment, betrayal, depression, and sorrow in the same way other people are. Such feelings are natural reactions to the experiences of life. But since it seems like a maxim of Christianity to "bear up under adversity," many Christians tend to deny such feelings. Other well-meaning people may try to comfort them, but their words are often more distressing than comforting because they too have the idea that the afflicted person must bear up in his difficulty. This may cause much damage by thwarting the normal process of grieving. Thus, the grieving person feels compelled to bottle up his natural feelings for fear of appearing to lack faith.

Because of their own fears, people sometimes try to keep others from expressing their feelings. If you are afraid of death, for instance, you tend to avoid thinking about that subject. Then if another person talks frankly about death, either his own or a loved one's, you feel threatened by his openness in expressing his feelings. It makes you so uneasy that you try to stop him by telling him not to be afraid and to have faith in God. But this is empty encouragement because it springs from your own discomfort about discussing death.

Expressing our true feelings to God is part of sincere prayer for the Christian. It is the pouring out of our souls (our inner beings) to God. He knows our feelings anyway, so why not tell Him exactly how we feel? Let us freely confess our anger, resentment, and discouragement, and let us also express our love, faith, and gratitude. We do not need to be ashamed to acknowledge our feelings of weakness and doubt, for Christ was touched with the feeling of our infirmities.

May we take a new look at the man Jesus Christ. He knows all our feelings because He was truly human as He walked on the earth. We can live with our own feelings of infirmity because Jesus understands and cares; He was one of us.

Chastisement

Why is life the way it is, with many things that seem unfair? One child is the son of a king, and another is born a slave. One child has a sound body, and another is physically handicapped. One is born with great opportunities for financial success, and another is born in poverty. Why is there so much suffering on earth, so much starvation, warfare, and oppression? Is this God's will for mankind?

"More Than Conquerors"

God saw that in our depraved state we would take our own way and rush to destruction if we did not face troubles and obstacles. These things are part of the curse that God pronounced on mankind. He permits them as part of His chastening so that we will turn to Him. Therefore, we should thank God for the hardships that we face.

God has certain things in mind, certain purposes that He is trying to accomplish in our lives. His ultimate goal is to free us from suffering and pain and death, but first He wants to deliver us from bondage to our own lusts and evil tendencies. Sometimes He stops us in our tracks so that we come to the end of ourselves and seek His face. But often we do not comprehend His workings, as suggested by the following stanzas from "God Moves in a Mysterious Way."

> Judge not the Lord by feeble sense,
>   But trust Him for His grace;
> Behind a frowning providence,
>   He hides a smiling face.
>
> His purposes will ripen fast,
>   Unfolding ev'ry hour;
> The bud may have a bitter taste,
>   But sweet will be the flower.
>
> Blind unbelief is sure to err,
>   And scan His work in vain;
> God is His own interpreter,
>   And He will make it plain.
>   —William Cowper

The Physical Body

The Christian is no less sensitive to pain and suffering than anyone else. People such as the Stoics have promoted insensibility to joy and sorrow, but this is neither manly nor saintly, neither virtuous nor blessed. Jesus Himself was keenly sensitive to pain and suffering; He was "a man of sorrows, and acquainted with grief" (Isaiah 53:3).

Faithful endurance of tribulation demands the strenuous exercise of spiritual powers. If we did not feel the pain of discipline, we could not derive any profit from it. Chastening borne in a right spirit and sanctified by God results in many rich benefits and blessings. It is grievous in the present, but "afterward it yieldeth the peaceable fruit of righteousness unto them which are exercised thereby" (Hebrews 12:11).

The best of God's children need chastisement, for they all have faults and foibles that need to be corrected. No wise father will wink at the faults of his children. He may disregard those of other children, but not his own. To be allowed to go on in wrong is a sign of alienation, not true sonship. Our heavenly Father never chastens in rashness but only in perfect judgment. "He doth not afflict willingly nor grieve the children of men" (Lamentations 3:33). He never causes His children to suffer unless it is for their profit.

Is it possible to avoid the rod of chastisement? Paul wrote, "For if we would judge ourselves, we should not be judged. But when we are judged, we are chastened of the Lord, that we should not be condemned with the world" (1 Corinthians 11:31, 32). This passage suggests that if we judged ourselves accurately, with no partiality, there would be no need for God to deal with us. Hence, the only way to escape the rod of correction is to escape all necessity of correction, and that is impossible in this life.

Some chastening is the result of a specific sin; for when we transgress, we produce the rod for our own backs. Then when we cry under God's chastisement, we cry from pain that we brought on ourselves. Here we must be very careful lest we resist and rebel against divine chastisement. If we stiffen our necks and harden our hearts, we may finally experience not chastening but being broken with a "rod of iron."

It may seem that our afflictions will destroy us, but the purpose for them is that we will not be destroyed. We may feel that we will sink under our troubles, but they are sent so that we will not be sunk. God troubles His people now for the sole reason that He need not trouble them hereafter. He smites them gently now so that He need not smite them later with the arm of destruction. By an unreserved trust in our heavenly Father, we can be "more than conquerors" even in the midst of severe chastening.

Suffering

Suffering is bound up in the curse resulting from the sin of man. Sin brings suffering; however, we could never suffer enough to satisfy the justice of God or to pay the price of redemption for our sins. God uses suffering as a way to show man the consequences of sin so that man returns to Him. Sin may have a long tether, and suffering for sin may be delayed; but suffering follows sin as surely as night follows day.

There are times when every nerve in us seems to be a

The Physical Body

channel of pain and when the body is submerged in a boundless ocean of misery. We feel like David when he said, "All thy waves and thy billows are gone over me" (Psalm 42:7), or like Job when he cried, "Oh that my grief were throughly weighed, and my calamity laid in the balances together!" (Job 6:2). Even a strong man cries for relief when he is in such a condition. His agony may be so great that he craves rest in the tomb.

No onlooker can determine the full weight of another person's suffering. Therefore, we should withhold judgment when the sigh of complaint escapes from the sufferer. Only the person himself knows the keenness of his pangs. Worn down, he cries for an end to his anguish. May we not increase his suffering with empty and insensitive words.

We have a marked inability to descend to the depth of another person's pain. It is only as we ourselves suffer that we can know what others feel. We must drink of the same cup before we can know its bitterness. Yet even though we have suffered in exactly the same way, not even the words of tenderest pity can effectually relieve the sufferer. Human words are often hollow; and even words of true sympathy, cooling and cheering as they may be, cannot alleviate the pain. They may distract the sufferer from his sorrow for a moment, but it quickly returns as a flowing tide.

The suffering heart of man has always longed to know why afflictions come. Even Jesus, our great example of patience in suffering, cried aloud, "My God, my God, why hast thou forsaken me?" Though sometimes there is an answer, we often can find no reason under heaven for the pain we endure. God may give no account of His ways, yet we can be assured that His purposes are all wise and good. Our faith must be tested, developed, and perfected by the trials and pains of this life. By the slow steps of suffering, we reach the heights of Christian virtue.

The school of affliction is a hard school, but its patient scholars are well taught. And though no affliction seems joyous in the present, "nevertheless afterward it yieldeth the peaceable fruit of righteousness unto them which are exercised thereby." Sorrow may be the means of evoking the most sincere and beautiful expressions of trust and obedience. The highest level of submission was attained by our great Pattern, who in the darkest affliction and sorrow cried out, "Nevertheless not my will, but thine, be done."

Suffering is sometimes the result of sins in one's youth. These can be forgiven, but some sins of youth bear fruit many years later; their consequences cannot be avoided. Therefore, it is great folly to live carelessly in sin while young, in the hope of future forgiveness and tranquillity. If we have done this, our only hope is to own our sins before God and show ourselves heartily ashamed of them. It is best to give God every hour of our lives; but if the early hours have been misspent, it is still possible to mend our ways and give God our best in our remaining years. Never is a case hopeless when a man sincerely repents and seeks the grace of God.

The right use of reflection on the sins of youth is to make a man humble and to move him to warn young men lest they also make the mistakes that have thrown a shadow over the years of the older one. For he who is converted in later years would surely give everything he has to go back and begin again and so avoid the past follies that have brought him years of shame and suffering. The sowing of wild oats is certain to be followed by a bitter harvest, sooner or later. There is very little comfort for suffering that we bring upon ourselves by our own folly.

Not all suffering has its roots in personal sin. There may be intense suffering in the very bosom of innocence, just as truly as frost may settle on the purest rose in a garden. Hence the riddle of human suffering is not to be read as men superficially read it, assuming that it is always the penalty for sin. Much suffering is and will remain a closed book, a mystery, an enigma. But to the believer in God, suffering is only the dark side of a cloud whose edges are silvered with eternal splendor. For there is no strength without trial, no wisdom without experience, no refinement without pain, and nothing of true value without a price.

Suffering has various, practical benefits for Christians. It helps us to cease from sin, to avoid returning to the sins of the past, and to grow in humility and obedience. Suffering helps to defeat the power of sin and Satan, to manifest the power and grace of God, to purify the believer as gold is purified, and to develop long-suffering and endurance. It is by suffering that we learn how to suffer, that is, to be patient in suffering.

Received and borne in a right spirit, suffering bears witness to the glorious truth that "God is love." God's perfect love in us dispels the fears associated with suffering. It inspires a holy confidence and a victorious trust in Christ, even as in the apostles who were "rejoicing that they were counted worthy to suffer shame for his name." May we triumph in the same spirit, as "more than conquerors" over every affliction.

Disciplined Life

There is a way of living which may be likened to a horse that lies down in the harness and refuses to move, and there is another way which may be likened to a horse that runs away and breaks the harness and smashes everything. The Christian life is found between the lying down and the running away. It is a constructive and disciplined life, a discipline of the desires. Our desires are the God-given forces of our personality and are right in themselves. Without desire, life would quickly vegetate. But our desires must be disciplined, or they will ruin us.

"Free grace" has been preached many times in such a way that it weakens character. But the apostle Paul instructed the Galations not to use Christian liberty for an occasion to the flesh (see Galatians 5:13). Many, however, have used it for that very purpose. They have turned liberty into license. The truth is that grace is a privilege—a blessed privilege—yet it is permeated with discipline. Many people accept grace and receive new life, but then it leaks out because of a lack of discipline. God will not pour His grace down the ratholes of undisciplined living.

Christian discipline begins at the center and not at the surface. The first requirement is an undivided affection. "No man can serve two masters: for either he will hate the one, and love the other; or else he will hold to the one, and despise the other" (Matthew 6:24). So discipline your heart to a complete surrender and devotion to God. Do not just give up this thing or that thing. Many folks surrender surface things but remain unsurrendered at heart. They care little about character and much about reputation. They could become great men and women for God if only the things they did were to glorify God instead of self.

Do not try to discipline an unsurrendered self; it cannot be done. It will result in sitting on the lid and holding down that which cannot be restrained successfully. You will defeat your own purpose because you will be giving self more attention than ever—which is exactly what you are trying to avoid. Even after we surrender self to God, it will continually seek to regain dominion over us. Therefore, we must make a once-and-for-all surrender of self and follow up with continual discipline to keep self subordinate. It is the law of losing one's life in order to find it.

The disciplined Christian is not free to do as others do, but free to do what others cannot do. He is not free to do as he pleases but free to do as he ought. He is free to be a contributing soul, full of light and power. He may be dammed up like a stream at one level, but only in order to raise his powers to function at a higher level.

You cannot have an undisciplined life and also a beautiful life. Worry is undisciplined foresight. Gluttony is undisciplined appetite. Lust is undisciplined sexual desire. Discipline, or chastening, brings life into controlled harmony by directing it toward great ends. "Blessed is the man whom thou chastenest, O LORD, . . . that thou mayest give him rest from the days of adversity" (Psalm 94:12, 13).

As we examine our lives, do we see anything that is incompatible with the fundamental surrender of self? Perhaps we have a habit that saps the vitality from the central purpose of life, such as taking the route of least resistance, trying to evade responsibility, or making excuses when asked to serve in some way. Or we may tend to be critical and faultfinding or to compare ourselves with others instead of with the will of God. Are we willing to use the discipline necessary to overcome these habits? It is the only way to make the progress that we are longing for.

We need to build up a set of good habits so that we take the Christian way without even thinking about it. Any repeated act will develop into a pattern of behavior that tends to repeat itself automatically. A good action is never lost; for even though it has no apparent effect on the other person, it does something for us and becomes part of the good treasure in our hearts. Likewise, an evil action becomes part of a store of evil that tends to propagate itself. Every time a person yields to temptation, it becomes easier to yield to the next temptation until his character is fixed in evil. The store of good or evil in our hearts will finally determine our destiny.

We need to discipline ourselves where temptation begins. In Matthew 18:8, 9, Jesus said that if your hand, foot, or eye offends you (causes you to sin), you should cut it off or pluck it out. So discipline your hand not to take hold of something unless you want that thing to take hold of you. Discipline your feet not to approach a thing unless you intend to make it part of your life. Discipline your eyes not to look at a thing unless you intend to participate in it. Anyone who thinks he can indulge at the place of looking and pull back at the place of doing is standing on a slippery slope. To resist temptation is much easier than

The Physical Body

to avoid the destiny that comes from approaching and handling the forbidden thing.

We need to discipline our use of time. Perhaps we have good intentions to do certain things, but we fail to complete them because we run out of time. If we actually do not have time for a certain thing, we should not try to do it—even something good. But the real problem may be that we fail to make the best use of the time we have. Do we carry on conversations long after they have run out of intelligence? Do we tackle our tasks decisively and get them promptly out of the way? Do we daydream instead of thinking? Do we dawdle instead of doing? Time is life; let us not waste it, for in so doing we waste ourselves.

We need to discipline ourselves to live in the present: to live on what is, not on what was or will be. When the children of Israel first received manna in the wilderness, they did not know what it was. So they called it manna, which means "What is it?" Later they grew tired of manna, but it sustained them until they reached the Promised Land. We too may get tired of what is, but we must learn to live on it until we get to the Promised Land. Not until we reach heaven can we live on what will be.

We need to have disciplined tongues. "By thy words thou shalt be justified, and by thy words thou shalt be condemned" (Matthew 12:37). If we tell lies, we become a lie. The greatest punishment for a liar is his own character; he must live with a man that cannot be trusted. So discipline your tongue to the truth. And discipline yourself to concise, straightforward speech. We often say less by saying more when we could say more by saying less.

The Christian life is a life of discipline and not merely

a doctrine, for doctrine apart from discipline is dead. Only Christ can conquer our selfish nature and implant His mind and character in us.

Growing Old Gracefully

Old age can be contemplated with anticipation and a sense of adventure. For it is from old age that we step off into the supreme adventure—the great beyond. It is our outlook in old age that determines whether it is a nightmare or a golden sunset. Life is happy and uninhibited where the aged have faith in God, are free from the fear of death, and are active. But if our spirits droop, our shoulders will also droop. If our souls lose their music, our bodies will lose their vibrancy. Therefore, keep your soul alive and growing, and it will keep your body alive until its work is done.

Do not fight the fact that you are getting old. You cannot be twenty-eight again, so make fifty-eight or seventy-eight beautiful and useful. Every age has its own peculiar beauty and makes its own contribution. Whatever age you find yourself in, love it. Decide that you would not want to be twenty-eight again. For the present life is so interesting and full of joys that youth did not hold, and you now have an undisturbed poise that you did not have when younger.

Accept the liberties that come with old age. Youth has its freedom, but so does advancing age. In many ways, you have greater liberty to love and help others than ever before. Take on the responsibilities that come through the freedom of advancing age. Even though you have spent many years with your children and they are grown up and

The Physical Body

gone, see what you can do for them and other children by way of encouragement and a godly example.

Make old age the most fruitful part of your life. "They shall still bring forth fruit in old age; they shall be fat and flourishing" (Psalm 92:14). Some people do their finest work in old age. If we are to have a beautiful and fruitful old age, we must decide that it will be so. It will not happen automatically, however pleasant the circumstances may be. We should grow from the inside out with such a vitality that our wrinkles will hardly be noticed.

We do not grow old; we become old by not growing. It is a grave mistake to assume that the end of physical growth is the end of all growth. If we heed the laws of growth, those laws will operate to the very end of life and beyond. We cannot keep from getting old by various devices of dress or paint; age will show right through such thin stuff. But the ornament of a meek and quiet spirit only grows more beautiful with age. God may discipline us with minor pains so that we tone up our lives against larger issues and thus live longer.

Old age should be a time of expectancy, not reminiscence. Some old people have daydreams like the blossoms on Aaron's rod. The reason they live in the past is that they have ceased to be creative in the present. An old person who is creative does not turn to the past except for reference, for he belongs to the present and the future. To learn lessons from the past is wisdom; to try to live in the past is folly. Even worse, it can be a self-made prison.

The opposite is to take flight into the future. Perhaps there is no past to glory over, and the present is frustrating. So the person lives in dreams that are always going to be and never come to pass. Indeed, there is glory ahead for the saint of God, but a flight into the future to escape the present will cause us to miss the beauty we could be enjoying today. We cannot just live in the hope of leaving this world and being with Christ; we must also fill the present with life and love.

Another approach is to detach oneself from surrounding life; to escape not into the past or the future, but to simply retreat in the present. Some older folks do this because they are fearful or uneasy in the present world. They may build illusions of grandeur and muse over their own ideals instead of taking part in the activities around them. This can only bring unhappiness and produce an unbalanced and frustrated personality. Let us face life realistically, using every trial and temptation, every pleasure and pain, every compliment and criticism in such a transforming way that they add grace and virtue to our old age.

In going from middle age into old age, many people live under a cloud that overshadows their inner poise and leaves an undertone of anxiety. It is the thought that the vitality of youth and middle age is ebbing away, to be gone forever. This can lead to a fearful fighting for life and its powers, which brings all sorts of uncertainty and insecurity. Such a struggle will consume even more of their energies and only hasten the decline they are trying to resist. The thing to do is not to fear or fight old age, but to accept it calmly and use it to the best possible advantage. Nature puts on her best robes in autumn and dies gloriously; she passes on with her banners waving. So you too can face approaching age with serenity and make your last years the most beautiful.

The Physical Body

Let us consider some specific pointers for making old age blessed and enjoyable.

1. Accept your age. Do not forget that the best is yet to come.

2. Seek to be useful. Try to make a contribution to someone every day. Life is worth living when it is lived for someone else.

3. Keep active. Do not retire; just change your occupation. Start doing something you have wanted to do for years but never had the time or opportunity. Sitting down in retirement will ruin you physically, morally, and spiritually. You may not be able to produce as vigorously as before, but still produce something. Regular exercise, wholesome food, and freedom from worry are important keys to a long and useful life.

4. Increase your spiritual activities. With your physical activities decreasing, you have more time for spiritual things. You can gather the world to your heart and broaden your influence through prayer.

5. Keep laying up a "good store." Read and meditate upon the Scriptures and eternal truth. Let your subconscious mind become filled with good thoughts, motives, actions, and attitudes, and it will be deep subsoil into which you can strike your roots in old age and blossom to the end.

6. Cultivate the spirit of gratitude. Let gratitude become a settled habit. Do not let your life grow negative; keep it positive.

7. Keep climbing to greater heights. Do not let yourself coast along. Expect to be still in the making as a Christian until you awaken in His likeness.

8. Develop your mind all the way to the end. Do something mentally stimulating each day; read something fresh; pray for new burdens. Above all, fill your mind with the Bible, and you will never be empty and alone.

It is said that the capacity of the brain is highest between the ages of forty and sixty. Then its powers decline slightly until age eighty, but they do not go below the level at forty. So rather than saying we have a poor memory, let us say we have poor attention. It will be easiest to remember and talk about the things of the past; but if you set your attention on significant matters of the present, you can also recall those things even in old age.

To grow old gracefully, let us remember that the reward is not in the beginning or in the middle or even ten feet from the end. It is at the very end! God will reward, not our success, but our faithfulness in doing His will. May we be "more than conquerors" all the way through old age, for we are very near the final reward.

Victory Over Death

"Yea, though I walk through the valley of the shadow of death, I will fear no evil: for thou art with me" (Psalm 23:4). To an unbeliever, death is the worst possible thing that could happen because it ends everything he is living for. Not so for the Christian. Even in death, he fears no evil, for Christ has conquered death. Jesus said, "I am the resurrection, and the life: . . . whosoever liveth and believeth in me shall never die."

As death came through sin, so victory over death came through the work of the Lord Jesus Christ. Since He has conquered death, we as believers need not die, though yet

The Physical Body

we die. This is like the truth that since Christ condemned sin in the flesh, we need not sin, though yet we can sin. As the believer's goal is not to sin, so his ultimate goal is not to die. Thus in Christ, the believer has completely conquered both sin and death.

However, death is within us and upon us; it is in our body. On the very day we were born, death began to work in us. We all know that we are traveling toward the tomb. Death not only exists; it also reigns. It can strike at our bodies, leaving us weak and sick. Its effect has not yet reached its culmination, but it is reigning nonetheless. Its aim is to engulf and destroy the whole body.

We must see death as our enemy and overcome it by the power of Christ's death and resurrection. As He conquered death, so we must personally conquer death even in this life. We should not ask God for grace to put up with the power of death; we should daily petition Him for strength to overthrow its power. Let us consider three ways in which the saint of God can triumph over death.

By the assurance that we will not leave this world until our work is finished. God is in control of life and death; our days are in His hands. Consider the many times that death threatened Jesus while He was here on earth. The danger passed every time, for His hour had not yet come. He could not die before God's appointed moment, nor could He die at any place other than Calvary. We too can have the confidence that we will not die before our work is finished, whereas "bloody and deceitful men shall not live out half their days" (Psalm 55:23).

Another example is the apostle Paul. The powers of darkness pressed hard for his premature departure, yet he always triumphed over them. When the Holy Spirit warned him of troubles awaiting at Jerusalem, Paul said, "None of these things move me, neither count I my life dear unto myself, so that I might finish my course with joy" (Acts 20:24). Paul did not know if going to Jerusalem would result in life or death; but whichever it was, he expected to finish his course with joy. He did not expect to die when his course was only half run.

By the assurance that we can face death without fear if it comes. All men have a natural fear of death. Job spoke of "the king of terrors" (Job 18:14) and of "the terrors of the shadow of death" (Job 24:17). Even animals are said to go through a terrible fear at the moment of death.

But Christ came to "deliver them who through fear of death were all their lifetime subject to bondage" (Hebrews 2:15). By faith in Him, we have no fear of death, for death is swallowed up in victory. "O death, where is thy sting? O grave, where is thy victory?" (1 Corinthians 15:55). This is indeed a great triumph, for even the "last enemy" of man has no power to terrify him.

A number of Bible characters demonstrated the absence of fear in death. Peter referred to his impending death with the simple statement, "I must put off this my tabernacle" (2 Peter 1:14). Paul was actually "in a strait betwixt two, having a desire to depart" (Philippians 1:23) and also wanting to remain on earth. In addition, hundreds of martyrs have gone fearlessly to their deaths at the scaffold or the stake, some even singing for joy. This demonstration of victory over death has brought multitudes of others to the Christian faith.

By the anticipation that Christ will return in our lifetime.

The Physical Body

The fact that He has not come for some twenty centuries means that His return is only so much nearer. Therefore, we have a greater hope of being among the ones "which are alive and remain" at His coming than any Christians before us. That thought should fill us with eager anticipation. A whole generation of believers will be changed in a moment from mortality to immortality, without dying—and we may be among them! That will be the ultimate triumph over death.

"Beloved, now are we the sons of God, and it doth not yet appear what we shall be: but we know that, when he shall appear, we shall be like him; for we shall see him as he is. And every man that hath this hope in him purifieth himself, even as he is pure" (1 John 3:2, 3). Let us lay hold by faith upon God's Word and trust Him to the end. Moment by moment, let us live for Him and draw upon His resurrection power to sanctify our spirits, souls, and bodies, and preserve us blameless unto the coming of our Lord Jesus Christ. Then we shall be able to meet Him as "more than conquerors" and to reign with Him in life forevermore.